REGIS COLLEGE LIBRARY
100 Wellesley Street West
Toronto, Ontario
Canada M5S 2Z5

THE NEW
BUFFALO

D1564005

THE NEW BUFFALO

The Struggle for Aboriginal Post-Secondary Education in Canada

BLAIR STONECHILD

REGIS COLLEGE LIBRARY
100 Wellesley Street West
Toronto, Ontario
Canada M5S 2Z5

University of Manitoba Press

E
96.2
S76
2006

University of Manitoba Press
Winnipeg, Manitoba
Canada R3T 2M5
uofmpress.ca

© Blair Stonechild 2006

19 18 17 16 15   3 4 5

Printed in Canada
Text printed on chlorine-free, 100% post-consumer recycled paper

All rights reserved. No part of this publication may be reproduced or transmitted in
any form or by any means, or stored in a database and retrieval system, without the
prior written permission of the University of Manitoba Press, or, in the case of
photocopying or any other reprographic copying, a licence from Access Copyright
(Canadian Copyright Licensing Agency). For an Access Copyright licence,
visit www.accesscopyright.ca, or call 1-800-893-5777.

Cover design: Joe Grande, Grandesign Ltd.
Cover image: Manitoba Borealis Bison, December 26, 2002,
La Broquerie, Manitoba, by Gill Gauthier
Interior design: Relish Design Studio

Library and Archives Canada Cataloguing in Publication

The new buffalo : the struggle for Aboriginal post-secondary education in Canada /
Blair Stonechild.

Includes bibliographical references.
ISBN 978-0-88755-693-0 (pbk.)
ISBN 978-0-88755-377-6 (PDF e-book)
ISBN 978-0-88755-413-1 (epub e-book)

1. Native peoples—Education (Higher)—Canada—History. 2. Native
peoples —Government relations. I. Title

E96.2.S76 2006   378.1'982997071   C2006-905052-X

The University of Manitoba Press gratefully acknowledges the financial
support for its publication program provided by the Government of Canada
through the Canada Book Fund, the Canada Council for the Arts, the Manitoba
Department of Culture, Heritage, Tourism, the Manitoba Arts Council,
and the Manitoba Book Publishing Tax Credit.

Contents

List of Tables

Preface

THE NEW BUFFALO focusses on identifying and interpreting key factors in the evolution of Canadian Aboriginal post-secondary education policy factors, including the rationale and nature of policy and issues of legislative authority, policy making, and funding powers. The issue of jurisdiction is central to First Nations post-secondary education policy and is examined in the context of federal and provincial roles and responsibilities, of university education generally, and in terms of the evolution of Aboriginal self-government. This work is the first major exploration of First Nations post-secondary education policy, especially in its attempts to discern the underlying issues.

Lacking other major historical studies of First Nations higher education policy, I have examined written sources in order to discern and identify the broad patterns of evolution in the overall policy. The Record Group 10 microfilms of the National Archives contain documentation on the earliest cases of Indians receiving assistance from Indian Affairs to attend universities. Annual reports of Indian Affairs provide information on the informal funding arrangements that began in 1957 under the Diefenbaker government. A variety of sources, including archival collections such as the

Blakeney Papers at the Saskatchewan Archives, provide insight into the policy discussions that surrounded the federal and provincial governments' response to the Indian Control of Indian Education policy. The Blakeney Papers shed light on the Province of Saskatchewan's important role in the early formation of the Saskatchewan Indian Federated College, as did the Lloyd Barber Papers in the University of Regina Archives.

I sought materials at the ministerial level through Access to Information at the Treaties and Historical Research Centre at Indian and Northern Affairs Canada in Gatineau. These included records regarding Manitou College at La Macaza, Quebec, a now-defunct First Nations college, and Indian Affairs dealings with respect to the protests surrounding capping of post-secondary funding in the late 1980s. Hearings of the Standing Committee on Aboriginal Affairs and Special Senate Committee on Post-Secondary Education provided a record of the views of the various policy stakeholders. I obtained documents and position papers describing First Nations involvement and positions from the Federation of Saskatchewan Indian Nations, Saskatchewan Indian Federated College, Assembly of First Nations, and from various news articles, including online copies of the *Saskatchewan Indian* newsmagazine.

While the study of Indigenous knowledge and its holistic approach offers a potentially valuable paradigm for modern thinking, I did not intend to examine such pedagogical issues. I wanted to analyze the political and jurisdictional environment of Aboriginal policy generally, and First Nations higher education policy specifically. Based on the results of my research, overall conclusions can be reasonably drawn concerning jurisdictional, legislative, policy-making, and funding responsibilities for Indian higher education, and what paths the various parties involved may pursue to resolve challenging issues.

I hope this work will sensitize the reader to First Nations policy in a broad sense, and will provide insight into the specific topic of First Nations post-secondary policy. Researching and writing the book has enabled me to address many questions that had arisen as a result of having personally experienced residential school, integrated urban high school, mainstream university, and First Nations-controlled higher education as a student, teacher, and administrator. I hope this work will provide guidance and encouragement to those individuals, too numerous to all be acknowledged, who believe in the power of Aboriginal-controlled higher education, the dignity it brings, and the promise it holds for future generations.

I am indebted to Dr. James Pitsula and Dr. Rod Dolmage, both of the University of Regina, and to Dr. Eber Hampton of the First Nations University of Canada, for their participation in my doctoral program, which resulted in the PhD thesis that provided the basis for this book. Organizations that facilitated my research include the Indigenous Studies Research Centre, Canadian Plains Research Center, First Nations University of Canada, and Saskatchewan Archives, all in Regina; as well as the Treaties and Historical Research Centre in Gatineau and National Archives of Canada in Ottawa. Gail Valaskakis, Noel Starblanket, and Bruce Sheppard provided me with interviews or communications that shed light on policy interactions, and former Saskatchewan Premier Allan Blakeney granted permission to access his collection at the Saskatchewan Archives. I thank Neal McLeod, Rob Nestor, and other colleagues at the First Nations University of Canada for their moral support. The quality of this publication would not have been possible without the assistance of David Carr and Pat Sanders of the University of Manitoba Press. My wife Sylvia provided invaluable encouragement, and my son Michael and daughters Rachel and Gabrielle gave me inspiration to complete the book.

Introduction

THIS BOOK EXAMINES the policy evolution of an increasingly crucial aspect of Aboriginal policy, that surrounding post-secondary education. First Nations higher education policies, including efforts to increase student access to higher learning, have evolved significantly. Although government programs designed to attract Aboriginal students to universities have resulted in increased participation rates, obstacles remain to making higher education culturally relevant and equitable. A solution promoted by First Nations is the creation of their own institutions of higher education. However, a fundamental policy disagreement exists between First Nations and the federal government over whether higher education is a treaty and Aboriginal right obtained in return for the sharing of lands. This book examines the need for enhanced recognition of the importance of higher education rights, and increases to institutional capacity, in order for higher education to truly be the "new buffalo" that will ensure a strong and prosperous future for First Nations. In the past, the buffalo met virtually every need of the North American Indian, from food to shelter; this animal was considered to be a gift from the Creator intended to provide for the peoples' needs. Today, elders say that education, rather than the bison, needs to be relied upon for survival.[1]

Understanding which level of government has jurisdiction and responsibility for the funding of Indian higher education is a daunting challenge. The issue is complex. The federal government has historically denied holding jurisdiction over the area and the *Indian Act* remains correspondingly silent in that regard. The federal government claims that post-secondary education and universities clearly fall under jurisdiction of the provincial governments. Yet, the provincial governments, on the other hand, view funding arrangements, particularly when located on reserves, as falling under the auspices of the federal government. As a result, they generally do not fund First Nations-controlled programs of higher education. Simultaneously, Indigenous governments are increasingly asserting their own jurisdiction over higher education, but are hampered both by the lack of recognized sovereign power as well as by the lack of adequate financial resources to build and operate their own systems. The policy community is complex, involving First Nations and their students, the federal and provincial governments, and various higher education organizations and institutions. The issue is a passionate one that has invoked protests, as it represents not only future opportunities for young First Nations students, but also the aspirations of their communities for self-empowerment.

The role of Aboriginal post-secondary education has evolved from a tool of assimilation to an instrument of empowerment. There has been a succession of policy phases proceeding from assimilation and integration to the recognition of Aboriginal rights and the struggle for self-government. As well, public attitudes towards First Nations policy have changed over time. Other factors that are germane to the issue of post-secondary education include funding programs for First Nations students, the efforts to gain recognition of higher education as an Aboriginal and treaty right, support for Aboriginal-controlled institutions, and measures to cut back program funding. The area of Aboriginal policy has witnessed the development of new policy paradigms. In examining First Nations higher education policy, this book attempts to situate the issue within the context of global Aboriginal policy development, wherever possible.[2]

In the effort to decolonize Canada's Indigenous history, it is necessary to understand how the ideologies and attitudes that underlie government policies have left their stamp. According to theorist Linda Tuhiwai Smith, non-Indigenous history is an invention of dominant society, written to exclude Indigenous values and views while claiming to be an objective and accurate portrayal of the chronology of events, when in reality it is a tool of domination.[3] Smith describes a variety of techniques that can be used to decolonize Indigenous history, including ensuring that Indigenous voices are heard, incorporating values, beliefs and cultural interpretations as manifested by oral history and other knowledge traditions. Research should be conducted in a manner that involves Indigenous peoples and respects their points of view, and uses names and words to strengthen the Indigenous expression.[4]

The lines of jurisdictional responsibility between the federal and provincial and First Nations governments regarding First Nations higher education are fuzzy, to say the least. Section 91 of the 1867 *British North America Act (BNA Act),* the constitutional document that delineates the current division of sovereign power and jurisdiction in the Canadian system, states: "exclusive Legislative Authority of the Parliament of Canada extends to … Indians and lands reserved for Indians." On the other hand, it can be argued that provincial jurisdiction over education, including higher education granted under section 93, applies to First Nations residing off their reserves. While the *Indian Act* contains statutory provisions for funding on-reserve elementary and secondary education, it remains silent about higher education.

The *Indian Act* shields the fundamental elements of Indian identity and property from incursion or interference by provincial authorities. At the same time, the courts have questioned the theory that Indian reserves are enclaves in which provincial laws have no force.[5] Regardless of jurisdictional questions, provincial governments have done little to develop policy for First Nations higher education, despite keeping federal transfer payments that are based on the inclusion of Aboriginal populations, leaving decisions regarding Indigenous programs to the discretion of universities and colleges. Individual universities tend to mount Aboriginal programs out of a general effort to provide curriculum relevant to Aboriginal peoples, rather than out of a sense of any specific mandate. The federal government has attempted to make the argument that the provinces should be playing a more direct role, but this argument is not viewed favourably by most Aboriginal peoples, who see themselves falling under federal jurisdiction. Hence, the main relationship in terms of developing policies and funding programs in post-secondary education has been between the federal government and First Nations.[6]

With respect to legal cases directly relating to First Nations post-secondary education, there have been few at the lower court level and none in higher courts. *Greyeyes v. The Queen* was the first to identify the federal government's responsibility for First Nations higher education. Courts can potentially play a crucial role in strengthening or weakening claims to Aboriginal or treaty rights.[7]

Since 1985, there have been numerous policy studies conducted by the Department of Indian Affairs on post-secondary education. Major evaluations conducted in 1985, 1989, and 1990 concluded that the program of post-secondary funding had brought about major improvements in Indian participation, and recommended ways to make the program more efficient. While these policy studies, which will be examined in greater detail in this book, have resulted in changes, they have not fully met First Nations needs. Aboriginal post-secondary education was also the subject of parliamentary committee hearings in 1989 and 1997, at which times First Nations voiced their concerns about funding and other aspects of the program. The draft Hanson/Macleod Institute report, commissioned by Indian and Northern Affairs Canada and released in August 2003, takes a broad look at the effectiveness today of the Indian Studies Support Program (ISSP), an initiative aimed at increasing support for post-secondary education. It concludes that First Nations-controlled higher education programs have made tremendous strides despite severe limitations on resources.[8]

There are few academic articles written specifically on First Nations higher education policy. Historian Winona Stevenson's "Prairie Indians and Higher Education: An Historical Overview 1876–1977" points out that the earliest role of Indian higher education was to serve as a tool of assimilation.[9]

Up until the *Indian Act*s of the 1920s, Indians who attended university could face automatic enfranchisement. Moreover, since Indians were legally wards of the government and under the *Indian Act* until 1947, they did not possess simple rights such as the ability to own private property or enter into contracts. Therefore, it was difficult, if not impossible, for them to pursue university education on their own accord.[10] Darlene Lanceley's "The Post-Secondary Assistance Program for Indian Education: The Vehicle for Change and the Voice of Opposition" recounts the Department of Indian Affair's measures to cap post-secondary funding in the late 1980s, and the opposition that resulted.[11]

There is a growing body of literature regarding First Nations aspirations in contemporary society in the wake of the entrenchment of Aboriginal and treaty rights, and regarding how new approaches can be envisaged for the future.[12] The *Tradition and Education: Towards a Vision of Our Future* three-volume report was the product of national consultations on education conducted by the Assembly of First Nations from 1984 to 1988.[13] The report took a comprehensive look at all aspects of First Nations education, including several case studies, and devoted significant space to post-secondary training. *Tradition and Education* made strong statements about the sovereign nature of First Nations and about their rights to control all aspects of their programs. This landmark study, which had been funded by the federal government in connection to the constitutional negotiations of the mid-1980s, became another policy input that influenced the development of the Indian Support Studies Program.

The five-volume *Report of the Royal Commission of Aboriginal Peoples*, commissioned by Prime Minister Brian Mulroney in the aftermath of the Oka Crisis of 1996, was the most expensive and comprehensive examination of the conditions and aspirations of Aboriginal peoples ever conducted.[14] The report surveyed various activities in the area of higher education and made several recommendations, including recognition of post-secondary education as an Aboriginal and treaty right, strong endorsement of adequate funding for Aboriginal-controlled post-secondary institutions, and creation of an Aboriginal Peoples' International University.

This analysis is not intended to compare Aboriginal higher education initiatives or programs in the different regions of Canada. As with issues of provincial involvement, such studies are beyond the scope and resources of this work, and are not essential to arriving at an understanding of the fundamentals of First Nations higher education policy. However, there is no doubt that Aboriginal-controlled higher education has become the aspiration of First Nations, as articulated in major documents including *Indian Control of Indian Education* (1972), *Tradition and Education* (1988), and the *Report of the Royal Commission on Aboriginal Peoples* (1995). Therefore, I place particular focus on the emergence of First Nations-controlled higher education as well as its importance to fulfilling aspirations of Aboriginal self-determination.

I use the term "higher education" to refer to university-level education programs. However, statistical analyses by Indian Affairs are in terms of "post-secondary education," which, in addition to university programs, also includes community college programs. I use terms "Indian" and "Native" as they predominate in the historical, legislative, and bureaucratic literature up until the late 1970s. The term "First Nations" begins to acquire meaning and usage in the period from around 1979 leading up to and after the Aboriginal constitutional negotiations, and especially when the National Indian Brotherhood became renamed the "Assembly of First Nations." This change reflected a growing nationalism and political consciousness among Indians, and communicated the message that their organizations were representative political entities, not just ordinary lobby groups. The term "Aboriginal" gained currency with its inclusion in the *Constitution Act* (1982) that entrenched recognition of Indians, Inuit, and Métis as "Aboriginal peoples." Finally, the term "Indigenous," which refers to originating from and having close ties to a certain land area, does not have any legal connotations but has gained currency in academic circles in Canada and internationally. This book deals mainly with First Nations higher education as part of broader post-secondary policy. While only modest references are made to the Métis or Inuit, the term "Aboriginal" is frequently employed to impart the message that government policy in this area needs to be construed in a much broader sense.

Chapter 1

Early Policies Regarding Indian Education

SOCIAL DARWINISM, a pseudo-scientific belief that some peoples, including Aboriginal peoples, were inherently defective in biological, intellectual, and emotional composition, was the prevailing ideology among Canadian elite at the time of Confederation. This thinking held that Aboriginal culture would not be able to cope with social and cultural challenges posed by the arrival of Europeans. These ideas strongly influenced government policy making, with the thrust being that the best chance for Indians was assimilation into the lower levels of mainstream society. Government administration was paternalistic and oppressive, especially in the West, where government embarked upon a program of aggressive assimilation through residential schools and undermined Indian efforts to retain their culture and defend their treaty rights. In the aftermath of the North-West Resistance of 1885, the Canadian government began to assert stronger control over the lives of Indians, particularly in western Canada.[1] Under such an approach, Indians were confined to their reserves, and, due to their legal status as minors under the *Indian Act* they were prevented from pursuing their interests, legally and politically.

In Indian education, the residential schools were intended to dismantle Aboriginal culture by removing Indian children from communities and subjecting them to cultural reprogramming. In general, Aboriginal peoples were deemed to be unready to undertake higher education. Despite this general policy, however, the federal government did provide assistance to a few promising individuals to attend university on a benevolent basis. Those who did succeed at obtaining higher education were considered ready for citizenship and became potential candidates for automatic enfranchisement under the *Indian Act.*

Englishman Herbert Spencer began to popularize the application of theories of evolution to human races in his 1857 publication *Progress: Its Law and Causes.* In this book, he portrayed the advancement of society from the simple to the complex as an evolution of its political, religious, and economic life. The key to such social evolution lay in its individuals, and it was here that the perceived lack of progress of Indigenous societies was ascribed to the inferior moral, intellectual, and social abilities of their members.[2]

The development of such ideas had begun even earlier in the United States. In 1849, the *American Whig Review* noted: "the scientific study of humanity, from being for a century back the theme of a few speculative philosophers, is become at last a topic of general and even popular interest."[3] Americans were faced with pressing racial questions due to the existence of Negro slavery in the American South, and because of the conquest of American Indians. Observations of physical differences among races became an acceptable basis for explaining racial differences. Phrenologists claimed that the brain of the Negro was said to be smaller than that of Caucasians, and thus: "The African race is, and has ever been, far inferior, in natural powers of intellect, to the white man."[4] According to the phrenologists, as a result of their evolution, Caucasians possessed superior "frontal and coronal portions of the head which contained the intellectual and moral organs."[5] In placing the various races on the scale of superiority, Negroes and American Indians, the "dark races," were situated at the bottom. However, it was claimed, "in the Negro brain the moral and reflecting organs are of larger size, in proportion to the organs of animal propensity ... than in that of the Indian. The Negro is, therefore, naturally more submissive, docile, intelligent, patient, trustworthy and susceptible of kindly emotions, and less cruel, cunning and vindictive, than the other race."[6]

For such reasons, and because of doubts about the adaptability of the race, the American Indian was viewed as being the least amenable to the influences of civilization. Prospects for their survival were seen as being bleak at best. In fact, it was commonly assumed that the American Indians would become extinct.[7] By 1850 the natural inequality of races was accepted as a scientific fact that was published widely.[8]

Interestingly, the greatest opponents of this theory were Christian denominations, who believed that drawing such dramatic conclusions about the fate of other races flew in the face of the biblical doctrine of the unity of mankind. Liberal thinkers believed that Indians had to be given a chance to prove themselves: "If the Indians still showed no improvement after being treated as human beings and in accordance with enlightened policy, it would then be time to say they were inferior."[9]

Canadians shared similar contact with the Indigenous peoples of North America, and were also acquainted with the ideas of Social Darwinism. Sir John A. Macdonald revealed his awareness in his May 9, 1883, statement to Parliament regarding the justifications for a residential school system:

> When the school is on the reserve, the child lives with his parents who are savages; he is surrounded by savages, and though he may learn to read and write, his habits and training and mode of thought are Indian. He is simply a savage who can read and write. It has been strongly pressed upon myself, as head of the Department [of Indian Affairs], that Indian children should be withdrawn as much as possible from the parental influence ... where they will acquire the habits and modes of thought of white men.[10]

Opposition Member of Parliament Mr. Charlton, questioning Macdonald, asked: "The evolution, I understand, is a very gradual one. Has the Hon. Gentleman any information as to the number of generations it will take?" In reply, Macdonald retorted: "I am not sufficiently Darwinian to tell that."[11] What was not in doubt were the Social Darwinist overtones in Macdonald's policy.

The role of Sir John A. Macdonald, prime minister from 1867 to 1873 and 1878 to 1891, in Indian policy is one of the lesser known facts of Canadian history. Biographer Donald Creighton makes scant reference to Macdonald's role as Superintendent General of Indian Affairs during the critical years from 1879 to 1887, implying that he played only a peripheral role in such matters.[12] Macdonald was co-premier of the Canadas with Étienne-Paschal Taché and George-Étienne Cartier in 1857 when he piloted through an *Act to Encourage the Gradual Civilization of the Indian Tribes of Canada*.[13] This bill introduced the idea of enfranchisement, which was regarded as conferring the privileges of civilization. The Indian candidates for enfranchisement had to be males of twenty-one or older, literate, and of "good moral character and free from debt." Historian Olive Dickason dryly noted that a great proportion of the white population did not meet these standards. Indian response to the 1857 *Act* was clear—only one individual had become enfranchised by 1867.

Macdonald did not play as visible a role in Indian administration as did departmental officials such as Lawrence Vankoughnet, Edgar Dewdney, and Hayter Reed. But it is very clear from reconstruction of policy making that the prime minister was responsible for the portfolio and ultimately oversaw the shaping of Canadian Indian policy. He played a key role after the transfer of responsibility of Indian Affairs to Upper Canada in 1860, and was involved in crafting Indian legislation and policy up to the post-1885 Resistance period. His vision for Canada was one in which the protections created by the British, including treaties and the reserve system created by Sir Charles Bagot, would gradually be reversed. Through enfranchisement and land surrenders, Indians would cease to exist as Indians as they became fully assimilated into Canadian society.

In 1860, under the *Management of Indian Lands and Properties Act,* Canada took over administration of the affairs of Indians from the British Colonial Office. The office initially fell under the Commissioner of Crown Lands, and Indian Affairs did not become a separate department until 1880.[14] In 1869, soon after Confederation, *An Act for the Gradual Enfranchisement of Indians* was passed that included a definition of "Indian" based on a minimum one-quarter Indian blood quantum.[15]

In the 1870s, the Canadian government's first major challenge in Indian policy was the process of negotiating the Numbered Treaties in the newly acquired North-West Territories. Canada was instructed to negotiate in order to fulfill stipulations of the *Royal Proclamation of 1763*. Under the proclamation, Indian land could not be occupied by the British until terms of treaty were agreed upon with the Indians. Assessing the situation during a visit to Rupert's Land in 1869, Secretary of State Joseph Howe wrote: "The Indian question was not presented to me in any form as I saw none of their chiefs, but they repudiate the idea of it [the land] being sold by the [Hudson's Bay] Company, and some form of treaty or arrangement will be necessary. Anything will be better than an Indian War at a distance from the center."[16]

An examination of the negotiations of the Numbered Treaties reveals that the Canadian negotiators, acting as agents of the British Crown, had wanted to concede no more than what was in the 1850 Robinson-Huron and Robinson-Superior treaties, mainly annuities and hunting and fishing rights.[17] The government tended to view treaties more as land-sale transactions than as commitments for ongoing relationships. This was the model of a one-time land purchase. In instructing the first Treaty Commissioner Wemyss Simpson, Joseph Howe wrote: "It should therefore be your endeavour to secure the cession of the lands upon terms as favourable as possible to the government, not going as far as the maximum sum hereafter named un-less it be found impossible to obtain the object for a less amount." Howe made special note of the "surrender negotiated by Mr. Robinson in 1850," which "had been a good bargain indeed from the Government point of view."[18] The government had received right of access to vast territories in northern Ontario in exchange for recognition of hunting and fishing rights and paying annuities. Promises of a long-term nature, such as providing education, health, or economic assistance, were not included in the 1850 Robinson treaties.

Hudson's Bay Company (HBC) officials had been giving warnings about the "war-likeness" of the Plains Indians. Canada opted not to challenge Indian ascendancy. The lieutenant governor of Manitoba and the Northwest

11

Territories, Adams Archibald, acknowledged about Treaty 1, "It was obvious therefore that we must yield something, or we must be prepared to people the country with hostile Indians hovering on our settlements, and an Indian war in the background."[19] Proof of this threat had been openly witnessed:

> A large number of immigrants who had made selections near the western border [of Manitoba], and who had been warned by Indians not to intrude on their soil till the treaty was signed, were in attendance and returned to their homes delighted to be able to put an end to the idleness of themselves and their families and teams, which their dread of the effects of incurring the resentment of the Savages had imposed upon them.[20]

Over the eleven days of negotiations for Treaty 1 (Stone Fort Treaty, 1871), Commissioner Simpson found anything but a compliant Indian population. He said "the Indians perceived the reserves as something markedly different from the Crown." In fact, they wished to retain for themselves two-thirds of the entire area of the "postage-size" Manitoba as their reserve. He told the Indians that "their demands were so preposterous that, if granted, they would have scarcely anything to cede" and urged them to curtail their demands.[21] By the fifth day, the meeting was at an impasse and the Indians were threatening to leave. Simpson reported: "During the night, active negotiations were carried on with the chiefs.... We acceded to their demands, and the whole matter was finally arranged at a meeting on Thursday."[22]

Commissioner Simpson had gone far beyond the terms of the 1850 treaties in order to provide an alternative to the Indians' insistence on keeping so much territory. Faced with Indian resistance to share their lands, Canadian negotiators found it necessary to make numerous other concessions, including provisions for education, economic assistance (agriculture), and later, medical care. Such an approach was more consistent with First Nations' desire to establish a relationship of ongoing mutual obligations.[23] These concessions took the form of a type of social contract, not unlike that which informally existed between the Indians and the Hudson's Bay Company.

Written treaty promises would include provisions for schools and teachers, to be established on each reserve. After much dispute, and the reviewing by Commissioner Alexander Morris of Wemyss Simpson's notes regarding additional promises not included in the written text of the treaty, a "Revision of Treaties One and Two" in 1875 was prepared that formally recognized some of these promises, such as agricultural assistance.[24] However, Indian oral tradition maintained that even more promises had been made, including tax exemption and medical aid.[25] Meanwhile, further west in 1871, Cree Chief Sweetgrass wrote to Manitoba Lieutenant Governor Archibald, "We heard our lands were sold and we do not like it. It is our property and no one has the right to sell them." Treaty 2, covering an area west of Treaty 1, was negotiated a few weeks later, with essentially identical terms.

The negotiations of Treaty Number 3, the North West Angle Treaty (1873), nearly failed over Indian refusal to relinquish their claim of ownership over land. Indians were well aware of the mineral wealth and need for transportation routes. The treaty took four years of negotiation, starting in 1869. The main Ojibway spokesman, Ma-we-do-pe-nais, made it clear that the Indians were conscious of the value of the land: "The sound of the rustling of gold is under my feet where I stand; we have a rich country."[26] The Indian negotiators managed to retain larger areas for themselves (reserves of 640 acres instead of 160 per family of five) and to secure larger annuity payments.

Treaty 4 (Qu'Appelle Treaty) was the first to be negotiated in "Indian Country," now called by Canada the "North-West Territories."[27] The militia from Manitoba, not the North West Mounted Police, as is often thought, were present at Treaty 4 as the commissioners' honour guard. The police had just arrived in Blackfoot territory and were beginning to deal with the American whiskey trading issue. The primary issue dominating the six days of negotiation again revolved around the issue of land and whether the Hudson's Bay Company had illegitimately sold the land to Canada. Negotiations had already been completed with the HBC, ending their trading monopoly in 1870 in return for £300,000 plus one-twentieth of the land in the "fertile belt." The Indians were hampered by political divisions, with the Saulteaux more skeptical than the Cree about the sincerity of government. This was likely a result of the ongoing controversy among their Saulteaux brethren about government failure to recognize the "outside" promises" not written into treaties 1 and 2. The Cree, led by Kakeeshiway (Loud Voice), were more amenable to discussing a possible arrangement that would be good for their children. Cree spokesman Kanooses sought assurances: "Is it true that you are bringing the Queen's kindness? ... Is it true that you are going to give my child what he may use? ... Is it true that my child will not be troubled by what you are bringing him?" A positive response broke the impasse over the treaty.[28]

Treaty 5, the Lake Winnipeg Treaty, was negotiated in 1875 in northern Manitoba because of pressures from whites for resource exploitation and rights of passage. This treaty was concluded relatively smoothly and included ensuring access to rivers and lakes for navigation purposes. However, in the next treaty, Treaty 6, Commissioner Morris faced much stiff resistance. One of the principal chiefs, Mistawasis had earlier turned back a survey crew and telegraph party. In 1875, the Canadian government had dispatched Rev. MacDougall to spread word that the Treaty Commissioners were coming. Cree chief Big Bear, fearing that there was something devious happening, told him: "When we set a fox trap, we scatter pieces of meat all round. When the fox gets into the trap we knock him on the head. Let your chiefs come like men and talk to us." At the Treaty 6 negotiations at Fort Carlton and Fort Pitt in 1876, chiefs Mistawasis and Ahtakakoop, who had been strongly influenced by missionaries, played leading roles. They approached Erasmus, reputed to be the best interpreter in the North-West Territories. This proved a wise move, since neither of the goverment's two choices for interpreter was competent in Plains Cree: Peter Ballendine was fluent in Assiniboine, while the other goverment interpreter, Rev. John Mckay, was mainly familiar with the Swampy Cree dialect. After Erasmus had left, because the negotiations were finished, McKay's effort to translate resulted in misinterpretation of Big Bear, making his motives appear to be criminal and casting his character in a poor light.[29]

Treaty 6 generated more debate and controversy than Morris had anticipated. Saulteaux from Treaty 4 tried to disrupt the proceedings and discourage the treaty because they had not yet seen any benefits. During their deliberations, recorded by Peter Erasmus in his memoir *Buffalo Days and Nights,* the chiefs challenged younger objectors such as Poundmaker, who was spokesman for Red Pheasant, to come up with a better solution. Poundmaker had exclaimed: "This is our land! It isn't a piece of pemmican to be cut off and given in little pieces back to us. It is ours and we will take what we want."[30] Facing such resistance, Morris was compelled to make a major concession, that of providing rations in the time of famine. In the treaty, however, the provision ended up couched in terms of a "general famine." The clause providing a "medicine chest," symbolic of the intent to provide health care, was also added. The Carlton area chiefs adhered to Treaty 6 on August 23, 1876.

The commissioners arrived at the second location of Treaty 6 negotiation at Fort Pitt, on September 5, ten days earlier than expected. They sent for Sweetgrass, a chief known to be sympathetic to a treaty, but not for Big Bear, a leader who had a reputation for being more independent and critical of white authorities. Sweetgrass would accept the terms with little debate. When Big Bear arrived at the meeting, it was already too late, and all he could do was to appeal to be heard and try to express his caution about the treaty.

At the Treaty 7 (1877) negotiations, Commissioner David Laird negotiated with the Blackfoot Confederacy (Blackfoot,[31] Blood, Peigan, Sarcee), whom the government feared would offer stiff resistance if not treated properly. One major issue at hand was to address the destructiveness caused by the presence of American whiskey traders. The trust that police such as James Macleod established with chiefs such as Crowfoot was instrumental in successfully concluding the treaty.

Sources such as John Taylor's "Development of an Indian Policy for the Northwest 1869-79"[32] and Ray, Miller, and Tough's *Bounty and Benevolence*[33] confirm that the Canadian government was not in a strong negotiating position when it embarked on negotiation of the Numbered Treaties. For this reason, these treaties contained concessions that did not appear in previous treaties in eastern Canada, in particular in areas such as agricultural assistance, medical aid, and schooling. All this was agreed upon at the insistence of the Indians. The federal government had hoped to make a simple land transaction and to avoid long-term commitments to the Indians. The government was aware that the First Nations had a history of strong military alliances. This was particularly true of the "Iron Nations," the alliance of the Cree, Saulteaux, and Assiniboine, a group that was well armed by virtue of the fur trade.[34] The white population, in contrast, was small, and the Canadian government had neither the resources nor the will to enter into a prolonged conflict with the Indians.

In terms of higher education, in Treaty 1, Commissioner J.A.N. Provencher, who had overseen the revisions to treaties 1 and 2 in 1875, suggested that the promise of education meant more than just the use of books and included "the intellectual, social and religious advancement" of the Indians. This suggests that the promise extended beyond merely elementary and secondary education.[35] When Treaty 4 was negotiated in 1874, it included the clause: "Her Majesty agrees to maintain a school on the reserve, allotted to each band, as soon as they settle on said reserve, and are prepared for a teacher."[36] This statement, however, did not do justice to the broader spirit and intent of the treaty from the point of view of the Indians, something that Commissioner Morris enunciated in general terms: "The Queen wishes her red children to learn the cunning of the white man."[37]

In Treaty 8, the commissioner reported: "They seemed desirous of having educational advantages for their children, but stipulated that in the matter of schools there should be no interference with their religious beliefs," suggesting that education should respect Indian culture. Such understandings also imply that the Indians who signed the treaties believed they were entitled to all forms of education, including higher education, as part of the spirit and intent of the treaties.

Today the courts recognize that the treaties must be more broadly interpreted and take into account Indian oral history. For example, in 1912, a main issue pursued by the Qu'Appelle Indians of Treaty 4 was to have "an Indian institution established where they can receive the higher education, so they can become Indian Agents, clerks and professional men."[38] It appears clear that the Indians expected more than just the basic elementary-level education that was provided in Indian schools.

In 1876, the Canadian government introduced its first national legislation, the *Indian Act,* modelled largely on the policy experience of Upper Canada and containing the practices developed under the British colonial administration. By 1877, Canada was faced by an approximately four-fold increase in the numbers of Indians because of expansion into the North-West Territories, and the need to reorganize and expand Indian administration was urgent. John A. Macdonald's return to power in 1878 came with a renewed commitment to complete construction of the Canadian Pacific Railway. Faced with the pressures of greatly increased Indian responsibilities and the unexpectedly high cost of concessions made to Indians in the Numbered Treaties, Indian Affairs was fashioned into a separate, larger department by 1880. Prime Minister Macdonald assumed the position of Superintendent General of Indian Affairs, ensuring his personal control over the Indian situation. He retained this post until 1887, after the upheaval of the North-West Resistance and effective control over the Indians had been established.[39]

While Macdonald clearly wielded control over Indian Affairs, he left its management to his close personal friend, Lawrence Vankoughnet, Deputy Superintendent of Indian Affairs from 1874 to 1893. According to historian Douglas Leighton, this mandarin was an unimaginative, penny-pinching bureaucrat whose sole concern seemed to be reducing expenditures. Commenting about Vankoughnet, Leighton states that his "personal inflexibility, his attitude of administration 'by the book' left too little room for common humanity."[40] Another of Macdonald's key bureaucrats was Edgar Dewdney, whom he appointed Indian Commissioner for the North-West Territories in 1879. Dewdney was a civil engineer and surveyor who came to Parliament as a member from British Columbia. His appointment was a reward for loyalty to Macdonald. By September of 1883, Macdonald ordered Dewdney to slash costs wherever possible.[41] Hayter Reed, Dewdney's assistant, who held some of the most extreme views of the time regarding Indians, later ascended to the position of Deputy Superintendent General of Indian Affairs. Reed quickly became Macdonald's key policy advisor and was instrumental in devising the repressive measures imposed on Indians following the Resistance of 1885.

Almost total insensitivity appeared to be the hallmark of government relations with the Indians of the West. In 1883, a letter from Fort Edmonton area chiefs described the utter destitution of their bands: "We were once a proud and independent people and now we … can get neither food nor clothing, nor the means necessary to make a living for ourselves ... the treaty is a farce enacted to kill us quietly ... let us die at once."[42] The letter failed to elicit any sympathy from federal authorities. On July 18, 1884, Indian Agent John Rae at Battleford, a relative of the prime minister, wrote a letter to Macdonald in which he bluntly warned: "If it is the intention of the Department to follow out their Cast Iron Rules then full preparations should be made for an Indian war. If the true cause of all these late troubles gets into the newspapers it will do no end of harm to the Government."[43] After receiving the chiefs' list of eighteen grievances from a Fort Carlton meeting on August 11, 1884, regarding everything from the lack of a school to poor health care, Macdonald perused the texts of the treaties but agreed with Hayter Reed's assessment that the Indians' concerns were baseless, and that the discontent was caused by ill-intentioned agitators.[44] Macdonald, in league with Edgar Dewdney, adopted a coercive policy of "sheer compulsion" in the months leading up to the 1885 Resistance, a plan they intended to enforce by means of the North West Mounted Police.

In February 1884, Vankoughnet wrote to Dewdney that "an example should be made of Chiefs or Indians who are guilty of such infractions of the law."[45] As a result, troublesome chiefs became the targets of police action. In February 1885, Macdonald authorized Dewdney to arrest and depose chiefs who were "agitators" and, in the process, to use whatever police force was necessary.[46] The numerous assurances by chiefs of Indian loyalty in 1885 seemed to carry little weight. Ironically, even Louis Riel, who claimed to be a defender of the Indians, revealed his Social Darwinist convictions when he wrote: "It is perhaps the one [the Métis] who, having enough white blood in his veins, honesty, experience, intelligence enough ... using his influence over them [the Indians] would show them how to earn their living.[47]

After the 1885 Resistance, twenty-eight Indian bands were portrayed as having joined in the uprising, and this scale of involvement cast into question whether treaty commitments had been broken. In reality, Hayter Reed's identification of "disloyal," bands was an analysis that diverged greatly from the reality. In fact, not a single chief had joined Riel's campaign, although individual Indian sympathizers did. Principal Indian leaders such as Big Bear and Poundmaker were unjustly convicted of treason-felony, a charge less serious than treason because they were considered to have been misled by Riel.[48] Macdonald played no small matter in these events, calling for the show trial that led to Canada's largest mass hanging of eight Indians at Battleford on November 27, 1885. He confided to Edgar Dewdney: "The executions of the Indians ... ought to convince the Red Man that the White Man governs."[49]

In typical fashion, Macdonald blamed the Indians for their woes: "It is a peculiarity of their race to be extremely susceptible to influence, to care little for the morrow if the day satisfies their wants."[50] Following the 1885 Resistance, the federal government imposed draconian measures that took away the Indians' freedom of movement, suppressed their traditional beliefs, and removed their children to residential schools. This went against everything that the Indians had heard the treaty commissioners promise. Prime Minister John A. Macdonald, as Superintendent General of Indian Affairs, expanded Reed's recommendation that "No rebel Indians should be allowed off the Reserves without a pass signed by an Indian Department official." He issued the directive: "The system should be introduced in the loyal Bands as well and the advantage of the change pressed upon them."[51] It is difficult to understand what advantage the prime minister thought the Indians would have, as the Resistance would dash the hopes of peace and harmony placed in the treaties. Macdonald would not make his first trip to western Canada until 1887, his last year as Superintendent General of Indian Affairs. There he repeated his goals for Indians in no uncertain terms: "The great aim of our legislation has been to do away with the tribal system and assimilate the Indian people in all respects with the other inhabitants of the Dominion as speedily as they are fit to change."[52]

The policy of aggressive assimilation was a radical experiment in social engineering. It was designed to quickly absorb Indians into the allegedly superior and more desirable British language and culture. By removing Indian children from their home environments and communities, in many cases for years at a stretch, the children were to become fully assimilated into white culture. Moreover, they were expected to be grateful for having been given the opportunity to receive such an education.[53]

Nicholas Flood Davin, editor of the *Regina Leader* and thwarted Conservative politician, was given a grant to study the impacts of industrial schools for Indians in the United States. His 1879 report led to the construction of three initial schools in the North-West Territories at Lebret, Battleford, and High River.[54] Indian residential schools became the primary federal policy instrument for the assimilation of Indian children in Canada. Unfortunately, the politicians and bureaucrats who devised the program had little expertise in education. Although funded by the government, the administration of the schools was handed to religious denominations, primarily Catholic and Anglican. Totally removed from their parents and communities,Indian children were subjected to a regime of inferior education and frequently spent long hours of labour to enable the schools to function within their inadequate budgets.[55]

The goal of assimilation that the schools were supposed to attain was never realized. School administrators were dismayed that Indian children seemed dull and unable to absorb subjects such as Roman and Greek classics. It only occurred to a very small number of teachers that there were serious language and cultural barriers, and that the curriculum was not relevant to the students' past experiences or future prospects. As early as 1905, both administrators and government officials already admitted that the educational goals of the schools had been unrealistic. At their peak in 1931, there were eighty residential schools in Canada. A survey in 1948 revealed that 40% of residential schoolteachers had no professional training. Many had simply been hired on the basis of "missionary zeal." It was no surprise then that the lessons were generally repetitive, boring, and not stimulating for the students, who responded with low academic achievement. This situation had been the product of a long history of residential school underfunding.[56] Unfortunately, however, the schools were very successful at destroying the cultural identity of the students, leaving a legacy that continues to damage First Nations communities to this very day.[57]

Indians had traditional concepts of "higher education" in which they undertook lifelong pursuit of specialized knowledge in order to become hunters, warriors, political leaders, or herbalists. Their education emphasized an holistic and balanced perspective of the world. When they came into contact with European society, their interests also extended to the pursuit of non-Indigenous knowledge and careers. For example, Francis Assikinack, educated at Upper Canada College, had aspirations of becoming a medical doctor, but was twice refused support by Indian Affairs. It was presumed such an endeavour would not have been a good investment of Indian funds by the department. Assikinack ended up becoming a frustrated schoolmaster.[58]

The first reference to enfranchising Indians (which meant giving up Indian status) who obtained a university degree, a reflection of official beliefs that possessing higher education gave one a type of independence such that he need no longer remain an Indian, appeared in Canadian legislation in section 86(1) of the 1876 *Indian Act:*

> Any Indian who may be admitted to the degree of Doctor of Medicine, or to any other degree by any University of Learning, or who may be admitted in any Province of the Dominion to practice law either as an Advocate or as a Barrister or Counselor or Solicitor or Attorney or to be a Notary Public, or who may enter Holy Orders or who may be licensed by any denomination of Christians as a Minister of the Gospel, shall ipso facto become and be enfranchised under this Act.[59]

This clause reappeared as section 99(1) in the 1880 *Indian Act,* section 86 in the 1886 *Indian Act* and section 111 in the 1906 *Indian Act.* The clause remained until the 1927 *Indian Act* when it was replaced by another clause that, although it did not specifically refer to universities, was actually broader in scope. That clause allowed the Superintendent General of Indian Affairs to appoint a board "to make enquiry and report as to the fitness of any Indian or Indians to be enfranchised, and such report shall have the same force and effect and shall be dealt with in the same manner as if the same had been made upon the application of an Indian or Indians under this section."[60] The above clause confirmed the continuing agenda of Indian Affairs to coerce Indians to enfranchise.

Duncan Campbell Scott, Deputy Superintendent General of Indian Affairs from 1913 to 1932, was a strong proponent of forcible enfranchisement. In 1920, he introduced Bill 14, which would allow the Deputy Superintendent to enfranchise any Indian he deemed suited, against that Indian's will. A committee set up to hear submissions on the bill held seventeen meetings and heard from thirty-five Indian representatives. The Indian response to the proposed legislation was overwhelmingly negative. In providing his rationale for the bill, Scott testified,

> I want to get rid of the Indian problem. I do not think as a matter of fact, that this country ought to continually protect a class of people who are able to stand alone. That is my whole point. Our objective is to continue until there is not a single Indian in Canada that has not been absorbed into the body politic, and there is no Indian question, and no Indian Department and that is the whole object of this Bill.[61]

Bill 14 was passed on June 25, 1921, and assented to on July 1 of that year. However, Arthur Meighen's Conservative government later fell, and new Liberal Prime Minister Mackenzie King, who had opposed the bill, had it repealed. As a result, Scott was unable to enfranchise any Indians under its provisions.[62]

A survey of annual reports of Indian Affairs during the late 1920s when Duncan Campbell Scott was in office did not reveal any evidence of enfranchisement of individuals who had obtained higher education. Those who enfranchised all did so for other reasons under section 114 of the *Indian Act* which awarded each a parcel of Indian reserve land. For example, in 1927–28, thirty-six heads of families took advantage of this provision.[63]

One example of an attempt to forcibly enfranchise an Indian believed to be too highly educated was the case of Fred Loft. Loft, a Mohawk who was born in 1862 on the Six Nations Reserve in Upper Canada, was one of those rare Indians who had completed secondary school.[64] Loft is particularly remarkable in that he personally led the movement to organize what would become the first national Indian organization of any consequence, the League of Indians of Canada. Meetings in 1918 on the Six Nations Reserve and in 1919 at Garden River, both in Ontario, drew Indian delegates from Ontario,

Manitoba, and Saskatchewan. The movement quickly attracted the attention of Deputy Superintendent General of Indian Affairs, Duncan Campbell Scott, who saw the league as a "Balshevik" [sic] threat and advised Indians not to have anything to do with it.[65] Scott interpreted Loft's statements opposing Indian Affairs policies in areas such as land surrenders and treaty fulfillment as a personal insult. He remarked in a letter: "I took a particular interest in this fellow's daughter at Toronto University and this is the sort of thanks one gets for it."[66] Scott resorted to attacking Loft's character and motives: "Mr. Loft is a physically good specimen for an Indian, but he is gifted with a smooth tongue, and a couple of years ago, being incited by the example of other Indian agitators, he set out to organize a society for the supposed benefit of the Indians of Canada. The collection of fees is to my mind the important part of his function."[67]

By 1921, Scott had determined that Loft's actions were a threat to the department and, after confirming his education and ability to support himself through working, determined that the way to deal with Loft was through forcible enfranchisement: "I fail to see ... why he should remain a ward of the Crown, if it is clearly established that his qualifications for citizenship are such that he no longer requires that protection." Loft was informed of the action to be taken against him.[68]

Scott, whose position as Deputy Superintendent General gave him extraordinary powers to implement this action, nearly succeeded, had it not been for the fact that his amendment to the *Indian Act,* which would have enabled Loft's forcible enfranchisement, was abandoned after the fall of the Meighen government in 1921. Had Loft become enfranchised, he could have been barred from residing on his reserve, a situation that would eventually lead to loss of connection to his culture and birthright.[69]

Loft's political activities, which extended as far west as Alberta, continued despite close scrutiny by authorities. By 1931, Loft had withdrawn from public activity for health reasons, and the following year, Scott retired after a lengthy career of fifty-two years with Indian Affairs. The shadows cast by Sir John A. Macdonald, Hayter Reed, and Duncan Campbell Scott over the Department of Indian Affairs were long. After Scott's departure in 1932, the department seemed like a rudderless ship, with few attempts at dramatic shifts or reforms in policy. The coming of the Great Depression in the 1930s heralded greater conservatism in policy and funding, resulting in a curtailing of many departmental services. This situation continued up to the Second World War.[70]

Indian Affairs annual reports made general references to Indians who had been financially assisted to pursue advanced studies in

> public high schools, high schools and colleges in Canada. In the case of most of these, the department assists with a grant from Parliamentary Appropriation. In this connection, $19,386.38 was expended during the past year. The policy is to make grants to the most promising graduates of Indian residential and day schools. If Church and department representatives consider a graduate worthy, the department provides a grant when the bona fide intention of the pupil is evident and provided proper supervision can be secured for the period of advanced study. These tuition grants are continued only when satisfactory reports are received.[71]

The department's 1926–27 report stated that "About 190 Indian students are studying high school, business college and other advanced work." No statistical breakdown of these numbers was provided, however.[72]

Indian Affairs had actually made earlier efforts to enable Indians to attend university, when, at the turn of the century, it found occasion to provide funding to some individual Indians who petitioned for assistance. Help was predicated on the idea that such aid would further the department's overall goals of promoting civilization. The first interest by the department in college-educated Indians appeared in 1902, in what appears to have been an internal initiative authorizing employee C.A. Cooke to gather information from various Indian Agents.

The Indian Agent at St. Francois du Lac in Quebec reported that, while he knew that some Indians had taken classical courses, he was not aware of any who had obtained a bachelor's degree.[73] Agent Bastien from Lorette, Quebec, reported that to his knowledge, Louis Vincent, who graduated from Dartmouth College in 1781, was "the pioneer of the Baccalaureat in America" among the Indians. As well, Paul Picard had graduated from Laval University in 1866 and was a notary public, and Rev. Prosper Vincent had earned a BA from the same institution in 1867. All three were residing at their reserves.[74]

In response to a request from Cooke for information, Paul Picard elaborated that he had commenced studies at Quebec Seminary in 1851, briefly attended Regiopolis College at Kingston in 1865, and then enrolled at Laval University. In 1876 he worked as a draughtsman in the Crown Lands Department in Quebec before retiring in 1892. He added that one of his sons had obtained a Bachelor of Letters at the Quebec Seminary.[75] In a further letter, Picard commented on why there were not more Indian professionals: "It is not lack of talent, but the means." He claimed that the government did not "acknowledge the many sacrifices they have had to undergo to become educated" and proposed that government should offer them positions, as "Indians have a better right to the liberality of His Majesty's government than any of the pale-faces."[76]

The Indian Agents at Roseneath and Walpole Island, Ontario, reported that there were no Indians in their areas who possessed a university degree. The agent from Sarnia, Ontario, reported that a Rev. Chas. A. Wells had obtained a degree from Victoria University, and resided at Lyons, Ontario. The agent at Hagersville reported that a Dr. P.E. Jones of Woodstock fit the category, but provided no information about where the degree had been obtained.[77] Josiah Hill of the Six Nations Reserve submitted a list of sixteen individuals who had attended institutions of higher learning, but the only ones who appeared to have completed degrees were Dr. Oronhyatekha (MD, Oxford), George Bomberry (MD, McGill), and T.D. Green (BApSc, McGill).[78]

David Laird, Indian Commissioner in Winnipeg, replied: "I am fairly sure that no Indian, treaty or non-treaty, has become a graduate … among our wards we may only count upon a few clergymen and school teachers, the qualifications and attainments of whom are considerably less than that of the average B.A."[79] A list dated January 15, 1902, apparently from the Archbishop of Rupertsland, added the name Rev. R. Steinhauer, BA. Finally, the agent at Victoria, British Columbia, reported, "I have not a few bright examples to offer you but, as yet, none have appeared amongst the Indians of BC who can claim that distinction [a degree]."[80]

In 1908, Joseph Jacobs of the Caughnawaga Reserve near Montreal was the first individual to petition the department for financial assistance, in this case to attend medical college at McGill University. Jacobs was a bright student, graduating with the highest marks from Fuller Institute in Grande Ligne, Quebec. His mother had passed away, and he argued that while he had started classes at McGill, he was unable to manage financially.[81] In his correspondence, he stated, "In reference to what calling I intend to follow when I have graduated, I wish to say that I want to take up the study of medicine and to advance my people in the way of education."[82]

After confirming the "industry, truthfulness or general integrity" of Jacobs, the department agreed to pay his tuition and textbooks, on the condition that the university supplied ongoing reports on his progress.[83] Interestingly, D.C. Scott, then departmental accountant, agreed with the recommendation, but skeptically noted: "this young man may be over-estimating his ability; but if this is so we will find out before long."[84] To the department's credit, it did stand by Jacobs when the student failed his course in chemistry and was forced to take a summer makeup class.[85] This continued to be the case when Jacobs ran into further academic trouble in two classes in the fall of 1909 and was forced to continue as a part-time student.[86]

By June 14, 1911, D.C. Scott was able to report to Superintendent General of Indian Affairs Frank Pedley that Jacobs had completed his arts degree requirements and recommended that funding be provided for the student to enter medical school. Scott noted that while tuition would be higher, the Jacobs family bore the cost of his board and clothing.[87] By 1912, however, Jacobs was petitioning the department for increased financial assistance "to that of a regular scholarship at McGill," adding, "I am the first Indian to graduate from McGill University."[88] The request was refused, with the observation that the department's assistance was already liberal. In the fall of 1913, Jacobs again wrote to Indian Affairs: "I am far from having enough money to keep myself in college this winter. My financial matters have been the greatest cause of my uncomfortness in college the last 6 years."[89] In reply, the department agreed to provide an additional sum of $100 per year, a not inconsequential sum at the time when a year's tuition amounted to $151. By 1915, Jacobs had completed his medical courses almost a year ahead of the usual five-year program.[90]

Later that year, Jacobs set up an independent medical practice at Caughnawaga. A letter to Duncan Campbell Scott reveals his experience:

> I have had a lot of work to do, but the unfortunate part of it is that there are so many poor people who are not even able to pay for this medicine [for themselves], and so not able to take the proper treatment. The result is I am already a hundred dollars in debt for the drugs. But what other course can I take, other than giving up my practice." [He concluded by noting:] "The prevalence of pulmonary tuberculosis among our young people is really alarming. It is a problem which I strongly urge you to become interested in.[91]

In response, Scott suggested that Jacobs should consider joining the army surgeons fighting overseas.

In the fall of 1914, the department received a request from Angus Splicer of the Caughnawaga Reserve, requesting assistance to attend Law School at McGill. The department agreed to fund Splicer on the same basis as had been done with Jacobs.[92] Splicer did not fare well, however, as noted in a report from the Dean of Law: "He has been relieved of the necessity of taking the examinations (which he would have certainly not passed) by going on active service [to fight overseas]."[93] Awareness of the possibility of Indian Affairs assistance had spread by now. In 1917, the Council of the Six Nations Reserve passed a motion requesting financial assistance be extended to Festus Johnston, a band member also attending McGill University, a request that was granted.[94]

In the West, the first institution for Indian higher education was Emmanuel College, established in 1879 at Prince Albert, North West Territories (today in Saskatchewan). Its purpose was to train Indians to become Anglican catechists, teachers, and interpreters.[95] Other than courses in English and theology, the Indian students also received systematic instruction in the Cree and Sioux languages. In 1881, a three-year degree in theology was added, and by 1883 the college successfully petitioned for a charter to establish a "University of Saskatchewan at Prince Albert." The university, which had been the idea of Bishop McLean, the founder of Emmanuel College, did not progress further after the bishop's death in 1886, and the college remained primarily a training facility for Natives.[96]

In 1889, the Anglican Archbishop of Saskatchewan sent a request to the Department of Indian Affairs for per capita grants for the students in its charge, on a basis similar to Indian children's being funded in residential schools.[97] "Training of native teachers" was described as the primary purpose for the twenty-four students enrolled at the institution. The petition was successful. Per capita funding of $100 per pupil was provided for industrial training, a stipulation from which Emmanuel College would later request to be exempted.

By 1895, the department raised concerns that the college "had not turned out any certified school teachers." In its defense, Principal Mackay pointed out that there was a "pressing need of school teachers compelling us to send them out before they were qualified to pass." He added: "Everyone acquainted with the Indian schools must know that there are no pupils to be obtained from any of the schools who know anything beyond the merest rudiments of an English education, and it must necessarily take a long time for even the most advanced to work up to the standard." In his opinion, some of the Indian trainees who had begun teaching without their certificate were proving more effective than whites with credentials.[98]

In 1897 agreement was reached to fund an additional thirty students but the department's per capita rate was reduced to seventy-two dollars, the same as for Indian boarding schools, which did not provide industrial training programs. A request for funding to expand the school's facilities was also denied on the basis that the buildings were church-owned rather than government property.[99] Consequently, the college continued to struggle financially and the failure of Indian Affairs to increase the per capita allotment or provide for facility renovation led to a crisis.

In a pointed letter of complaint, Principal John Taylor claimed that the task the college was performing came "as near as we can to solving the problem of how to teach the Indian to become self-sufficient, viz. by book knowledge." With reference to industrial schools, he noted: "After paying a large per capita grant every year in training carpenters, blacksmiths, boot-makers, printers, etc.—all this is found to be a failure."[100] A campaign to back the college's demands was mounted in Prince Albert by local Member of Parliament Davis and culminated in a petition signed by local community leaders.

In a subsequent letter, Taylor elaborated on his views of unfair government treatment of Emmanuel College:

> I was present when Treaty One was made.... Now as regards Indian education, the government is pledged under its treaties with the Indians to maintain schools on the reserves. But so inadequate has been the provision made ... that the church was compelled to start boarding schools.... Our church has in the past spent many thousands of dollars on the building and equipment in this institution and the building and the 300 acres of land on which the buildings stand have practically been handed over to the Indian Department as an Indian training school ... it is impossible for our church to continue to spend the large sums hitherto spent on this institution.[101]

Internal department correspondence revealed a perception that the institution had failed in its mission and did not deserve greater support. However, evidence had been produced by the college to demonstrate slow but certain progress. Of three students in form six, the last stage required prior to obtaining a teaching certificate, one student, Edward Ahenakew, maintained an average of 95% and another student, Alex Ahenakew, had an average of 90%. "We do not need to be ashamed of the progress that has been made at Emmanuel College," the principal concluded.[102] The Rev. Edward Ahenakew later became a prominent Saskatchewan Indian leader and educator. Unfortunately, the failure of Indian Affairs to recognize the value of Emmanuel College led to its eventual demise by 1923.

Chapter 2

Indian Higher Education and Integration

FOLLOWING THE SECOND WORLD WAR, the ideology of Social Darwinism began to fall out of favour. At a global level, advanced countries were developing policies to protect the rights and interests of minorities, and human rights legislation was being put in place. In Canada, successive federal governments were also reviewing outdated policies toward the Native people. Indian people were now invited to present their views, but their role still remained largely a token one. Under the Diefenbaker government, Indian Affairs began to implement a program of scholarships to encourage Indians to pursue higher education in order to help them integrate into mainstream society.

In his study of the formation of Indian policy from 1943 to 1963, historian John Leslie described the years after the Second World War as a significant learning period in Indian policy formulation. The period began with abysmal socio-economic conditions on Indian reserves and an Indian Affairs department bereft of ideas and inspiration. The policy community expanded through consultation with non-governmental interest groups, such as churches, and with Indians themselves. However, the department retained policy-making power and Indians remained on the margins as "policy takers," receiving but never influencing decisions. Leslie characterizes the shift in policy during this period as moving from one of open assimilation to one of integration, with the latter essentially being a modification of the former.[1] "Assimilation" described a process where services to Indians would become the same as for all other Canadians, with no distinctions being made. "Integration" would be a slower process, where Indians would be gradually encouraged to enter mainstream society on a basis of consultation and without coercive measures being imposed.[2]

Following the retirement of Duncan Campbell Scott in 1932,[3] Indian Affairs administration stagnated. Indian contact with the department was discouraged through means such as a 1933 ban on Indian travel to Ottawa, a measure intended to stifle Indian political opposition.[4] Government also reduced expenditures during the Great Depression of the 1930s and, by 1939, attention was focussed on the Second World War effort. By 1943, Indians began to organize on their own to protest issues, including compulsory military service. Nascent political groups such as the Indian Nation of North America, formed in 1945, pressed for recognition of Indian treaties and of the Royal Proclamation of 1763.[5]

One of the effects of the Second World War on the approximately 6000 Aboriginal veterans who fought, and on the Euro-Canadians who came into contact with them, was the realization that the liberty for which the war was fought did not exist for them. They could not allow this inequity to continue unchallenged. The 1947 Joint Committee of the Senate and House of Commons subcommittee hearings on Indian Affairs resulted in a series of sweeping recommendations for change. Education was one of the main topics of discussion, and concerns included the problems at Indian residential schools. One recommendation was to allow access by Indian students to provincial schools. These changes eventually led to the dismantling of the worst aspects of the Indian administration system, such as the restriction on Indian movement outside reserves, and ending the autocratic control of Indian agents.[6] Immediately after the war, however, Indians were still at a nascent level of political organization, and faced many disadvantages, such as the lack of funding in their efforts to influence government policies. These postwar discussions set the backdrop to the Diefenbaker era.

In 1958, the Diefenbaker government was elected largely out of desire for change. Diefenbaker's campaign featured a new vision of economic prosperity based on exploitation of Canada's northern hinterland, and a pledge to protect the human rights of the ordinary citizen, especially those from minority and oppressed backgrounds.[7] The large number of Aboriginal people in Diefenbaker's constituency provided a strong incentive for him to address their specific problems and raise their issues to a higher profile. One of the most basic rights, which Indians had not yet achieved, was the right to vote in federal elections. This was a matter that Diefenbaker was able to address relatively easily, as it was an area of exclusive federal jurisdiction and did not require wrangling with the provinces.

Undoubtedly, Diefenbaker also felt some pressure to compete with the progressive measures proposed by T.C. Douglas's Saskatchewan Co-operative Commonwealth Federation (CCF) government.[8] In 1956, wishing to be perceived as progressive on Indian issues, the CCF adopted an Indian policy based on three planks: extension of the provincial franchise; removal of restrictions on sale of alcohol to Indians; and transfer of responsibility over Indians from the federal to provincial governments.[9] Provincially, however, Indian leaders were not persuaded that Premier Douglas would be a strong defender of their treaty rights.[10] For example, in 1958, CCF minister John Sturdy, responsible for Indians and Métis, stated about Treaty 4: "This seemingly insurmountable roadblock towards progress of the Indian people must be removed."[11] This implied that the province supported total Indian assimilation.

By 1960, Prime Minister Diefenbaker had extended the federal vote to Indians, ending this aspect of their second-class citizenship.[12] The Diefenbaker government also drafted a bill for the creation of an Indian Claims Commission, to be tabled in the spring 1963 sitting of the House of Commons. The idea was not a new one. The 1947 Joint Committee of the Senate and House of Commons had concluded that Indian land grievances were an overdue matter that should be resolved. However, Diefenbaker's proposed commission would be extremely limited in scope; its main goal would be appeasement of perceived injustices, and its rulings would not be binding. However, plans to introduce the bill failed when the Diefenbaker government fell in 1963.[13]

Another initiative that had started during the Diefenbaker regime was the study of Indian socio-economic conditions. The International Order of the Daughters of the Empire approached Indian Affairs Minister Richard Bell in 1963 with a request that the government study ways in which Indians could achieve equality with the rest of Canadians.[14] The department was successful in securing government funding for a national survey of Indians. Harry Hawthorn, an anthropologist who had completed a recent study on Indians in British Columbia, was hired to conduct the project. Heading a team of fifty researchers, he demonstrated what most Canadians suspected, that extreme disparities existed. The average annual income of Indians was only $300, compared to that of $1400 for all Canadians.[15] The education statistics were equally dismal, indicating a dropout rate that resulted in virtually no high school graduates. The Hawthorn report noted that the main focus of existing adult education was on upgrading programs.[16] The report urged Indian Affairs to make available a wider array of vocational training programs, including access to university education.[17] The main reason for such broader initiatives would be to allow Indians to become more independent, as well as to enable them to better adapt to mainstream society.[18]

One of the most surprising outcomes of the Hawthorn report was a series of revelatory policy suggestions. Hawthorn concluded that the government had no right to limit the opportunities of Indians, including whether they should be assimilated against their wishes. Hawthorn determined that Indians had "special status" and that "Indians can and should retain the special privileges of their status while enjoying full participation as provincial and federal citizens." He referred to Indians as "Citizens Plus."[19] The report accused the Indian Affairs department of being "parochial" and "isolationist."[20] While provincial premiers such as Saskatchewan's Tommy Douglas had indicated a desire for greater provincial involvement in the affairs of Indian people, there was little federal-provincial cooperation in terms of program delivery. The responsibilities of provinces were now being brought into greater focus, as the provinces administered welfare, "to which all Canadians are entitled."[21] The timing of the report was auspicious, as it was released on the heels of Prime Minister Lester Pearson's declaration of his "war on poverty" in 1965.

———•◦•———

As part of Lester Pearson's "consultative federalism," promised in his election in 1963, Indian administration was placed on the agenda of a federal-provincial conference on finances. One of the outcomes of this discussion was the development of federal-provincial shared-cost agreements; Indian Affairs was beginning to spend in areas considered to be provincial jurisdiction, such as education and welfare, and concern had been expressed about duplication of services. There would be no extension of provincial services to Indians living on reserves, as Indian Affairs created its own program of welfare payments.[22] This was also consistent with the general expansion of the Canadian welfare state in the 1960s.[23] The Community Development Program, which was funded exclusively by Indian Affairs and was aimed at on-reserve Indians, was intended to train individuals to assist in developing self-reliance at the community level.[24] The result, in many cases, however, was a backlash demanding the department relinquish control over Indian communities. This situation produced such turmoil that the department terminated the program after two years of operation.

In an attempt to open lines of communication with Indians, the Department of Indian Affairs established a National Indian Advisory Board in 1966. The board included outspoken Indian individuals who, it was expected, would voice the views of their people on issues of *Indian Act* amendments and long-term planning. However, board members did not see themselves as having a mandate to represent their own people, and criticized Indian Affairs for not consulting directly with Indian communities. The board was dismantled in 1969 when members such as Harold Cardinal, president of the Indian Association of Alberta, rejected the board as a means of formulating Indian policy.[25]

Prime Minister Pearson agreed with Diefenbaker that the creation of an Indian Claims Commission was necessary because Indian confidence in the white man's justice system would be eroded if government did not seem to be willing to honour its promises.[26] Arthur Laing, Minister of Indian Affairs, estimated that total claims would amount to no more than $17 million.[27] However, when he consulted the Indians, he was met with a barrage of objections about both the nature and admissibility of claims. It was apparent to them that any fundamental notion of Indian rights would not be considered, and only lapses in obvious commitments would be resolved. The commission was doomed to be shelved again.[28]

Meanwhile, the National Indian Council, many of whose members were young Indian university graduates, had been founded in Regina in 1961 under the leadership of Indian lawyer William Wuttunee.[29] Its goal was largely cultural: "to promote unity among Indian people, the betterment of people of Indian ancestry in Canada, and to create a better understanding of the Indian and non-Indian relationship."[30] Organizational travel was generally at members' cost. One of the council's higher profile activities was advising on the Canadian Indian pavilion, a victory for promoting Aboriginal awareness at the Expo 67 World's Fair.[31] Although the pavilion was created under the Department of Indian Affairs, it provided a prominent platform from which Indians could express their dissatisfaction. In 1968, the Council split into the National Indian Brotherhood (NIB) and the Canadian Métis Society.[32] As the Pearson era came to a close, pressure had been increasing to take meaningful steps to deal with Aboriginal problems, and to go beyond simply amending the *Indian Act*.

When Pierre Elliot Trudeau swept into power in 1968, one of his main priorities was to improve government efficiency and policy making. In the case of Indian Affairs, he saw a department that seemed notoriously bereft of effective decision-making ability. The departmental bureaucracy itself appeared to be one of the main stumbling blocks to progress, but the fact that most ministers of Indian Affairs had stayed in the unpopular portfolio for less than a year meant they could hardly learn about the problems, let alone provide direction to the department. Under Lester Pearson, for example, Guy Favreau held the post for only ten months, René Tremblay for one year, John Nicholson for ten months, and Jean Marchand for nine months.[33]

Trudeau could hardly be considered a supporter of any concept of Indian "special status." Convinced that notions of special status being advocated by Quebec nationalists would seriously jeopardize Canadian federalism, Trudeau did not look favourably upon any special recognition for Indians. In a philosophy amounting to a type of cultural Darwinism, he believed that cultures should be allowed to thrive or perish as fate would dictate, and that this was the most natural way for society to evolve.[34] He summed up his view during the 1968 election campaign: "I am against any policy based on race or nationalism."[35] As for the long and complex history between Indians and Canada, and rights implied by the relationship, he was dismissive: "no society can be built in [sic] historical might-have-beens."[36]

Trudeau had promised to bring about "real change" in approaches to long-standing difficulties, and the "Indian problem" was high on his list. More progressive thinkers involved in examining the policy options believed that the Department of Indian Affairs was too entrenched to be capable of overseeing dramatic change. During the summer of 1968, the Cabinet Committee on Social Issues was considering Indian policy initiatives.

The Liberal government embarked on a series of eighteen nationwide consultation meetings with Indians, beginning in Yellowknife on July 25, 1968. The emphasis, laid out in a discussion paper entitled "Choosing a Path," was on equality of opportunity and self-help.[37] During the meetings, Jean Chretien, who had been appointed Minister of Indian Affairs in June 1968, was careful not to make specific comments about the direction government planned to take. With the appearance of meaningful consultation, the meetings raised Indian expectations, and gave them a real opportunity to reflect on their national situation.[38]

Vocal Indian leaders such as Harold Cardinal, who had studied at Carleton University, were making their positions heard and were calling upon the federal government to recognize Indian priorities. Cardinal called for reduction of the role and influence of Indian Affairs, acknowledgement of Aboriginal and treaty rights, and cooperation with the newly formed

National Indian Brotherhood.[39] When Parliament opened in September 1968, the desire to once again establish an Indian Claims Commission was mentioned in the throne speech. Beyond that, there was only a brief mention that Parliament would be asked to consider "measures relating to Indians," among several other matters.[40]

In the Prime Minister's Office, efforts were underway to synthesize Indian policy in a global and dramatic fashion. Brainstorming generated a series of ideas, including, for the first time, the notion of termination of Indian status, a sort of mass enfranchisement of Indians. Another idea considered was making available a large sum of money to assist Indians during the transition period to assimilation. These talks were secret, however, as they were not to impede the Indian consultation process. There was often confusion in the policy planning because Jean Chretien insisted on control over the process, while at the same time sending minister-without-portfolio Robert Andras to conduct the consultations.[41]

Under pressure from Prime Minister Trudeau in early 1969 for a document to present to Parliament, Chretien stated his conviction that whatever the policy was, Indians should be allowed to make their own choices and mistakes, like everyone else. This direction was confirmed in a Cabinet Social Policy Committee meeting in which a general policy objective of "full non-discriminatory participation" for Indian people in Canadian society was agreed upon.[42]

With the assistance of the Department of Indian Affairs, the Indian Policy was cast in specific measures, including the repeal of the *Indian Act* dismantling Indian Affairs, settling outstanding Indian claims and grievances, and negotiating with the provinces for the extension of their services to Indians. The process of drafting the policy paper moved ahead swiftly. Cabinet approved the policy, without Indian concurrence, and it was tabled in the House of Commons on June 25, 1969. In his brief address, Chretien characterized the policy as being a response to Indian concerns.[43]

Predictably, Indian leaders greeted the announcement of the new policy with disbelief. This feeling was compounded by the sense of betrayal given the process of the Indian consultations. Harold Cardinal would later comment: "Which Indian asked for an end to the treaties, which Indians asked for an end to their reserves?"[44] Other leaders were more blunt, shouting "Liar, liar" at Indian Affairs Minister Chretien. Opposition became so intense by July that he felt compelled to declare, "We will not push anything down anyone's throat."[45]

Prime Minister Trudeau preferred to leave the controversy to Chretien to handle, but, when cornered about the debate, he denied the idea of special rights: "It's inconceivable I think that in a given society, one section of the society have a treaty with the other section of the society. We must all be equal under the laws."[46] In a move that reflected a recommendation of the termination policy, Dr. Lloyd Barber was appointed Indian Claims Commissioner before the end of the year.[47]

The official Indian response, in the form of the Indian Association of Alberta's *Citizens Plus,* also known as the "Red Paper," was presented to Cabinet on June 4, 1970. Point by point, Indians reiterated their opposition and proposed alternate positions that would enhance their status. The paper proposed that Indian Affairs be terminated and that Indian communities assume responsibility for their own administration. It argued that Indian people had a living culture and did not intend it to be relegated to museums. They proposed revitalization of the relationship between Indians and the rest of Canada, based on recognition of treaties and Aboriginal rights.[48] The media coverage of Indian peoples from all over Canada, who were suddenly nationally organized, had a strong impact on Trudeau and on the general public.

In a spontaneous and surprising reply, the prime minister admitted he had made mistakes: "We had perhaps the prejudices of small 'l' liberals and white men who thought that equality meant the same law for every-body.... But we have learned in the process that perhaps we were a bit too theoretical, we were a bit too abstract."[49] The policy was officially shelved in March 1971. If one major lesson had been learned, it was that positive change could come about only with the cooperation of Indians, and paternalistic solutions were no longer appropriate. Another hurdle still remained, however. The government's position on Aboriginal rights still had not fundamentally changed.

One of the first areas in which the issue of the Indian right to self-determination would be tested was in the area of education. Residential schools were one of the most obvious symbols of paternalism, and, by 1965, Indian Affairs commenced the process of closing them. The policy shifted, without consulting Indian people, to entering into Joint Schools Agreements with local provincial school boards. In the cases where residential schools still existed, students would be bused to local white schools as residential schools were gradually phased out. The program had strong similarities to the Black desegregation initiative in the United States.

The Joint Schools Agreement signed with Saskatchewan in 1969 gave the province sweeping control over "schools in which Indian children are enrolled ... employment and supervision of teaching personnel and all matters relating to the curriculum." It went further to empower provincial school boards to assume control over federally run schools.[50] Examples of specific measures included an expansion of 200 spaces at North Battleford Collegiate at a cost of $220,000; 226 spaces at Turtleford School for $723,000; and 200 spaces at Carlyle School at a cost of $218,000. Altogether, from 1965 to 1972, a total of 6424 spaces were created at 61 provincial schools at a total cost of $7,692,993.[51] Many Indian communities wondered about the benefits for their students. A study conducted by the Federation of Saskatchewan Indians in 1973 found that only 5% of Indian students completed Grade 12, and less than 1% of Indians had completed post-secondary education.[52]

Joint school agreements quickly proved to be unsatisfactory as Indian students generally felt misunderstood, unwelcomed, and poorly supported. This, along with the threat to close residential schools, led to increasing demands for Indian control over their education. Indian parents occupied the Blue Quills School in Alberta and the Qu'Appelle Residential School in Saskatchewan.[53] In the first such case, Indian Affairs Minister Jean Chretien overrode his own advisors and challenged the Saddle Lake Band to take over running Blue Quills School.[54] These actions resulted in the first cases of Indian control over Indian education. Soon, Indian bands would be requesting that the relatively lavish amounts of money being spent on joint schools be redirected towards improving schooling in their own communities. These requests were eventually successful.

The raising of the issue of Indian aspirations was undoubtedly related to the coming to power of Prime Minister John Diefenbaker in June 1957, and this applied in the area of higher education, as well. Diefenbaker, who had been strongly impressed by Indians in his youth, considered himself to be a friend of the Indians.[55] In September 1957, Indian Affairs had begun to explore a system of higher education scholarships ranging from $250 for tuition to $1750 for "full maintenance." The scholarships were instituted as incentives to gifted Indian students wishing to enter university for teacher training, nursing, and similar programs. The 1957–58 annual report of Indian Affairs reported: " A system of scholarships amounting to $25,000 was instituted to act as an incentive to outstanding students. To be awarded for the first time in September 1957, these scholarships will enable the winning students to continue their studies at universities or in teachers' colleges, or at nursing schools, technical or agricultural schools."[56] (But by 1963 only twenty-two scholarships totaling $40,000 had been awarded.[57]) Prime Minister Diefenbaker sometimes personally presented the scholarships to Indian university students. Despite the challenges of cultural adaptation, many of these students were able to successfully complete their programs because they were highly capable and motivated. The first statistical breakdown of numbers of Indians attending universities appeared in the department's annual report for 1957–58 (see Table 1).

TABLE 1: Enrolment of Indians in Professional Courses, 1956–58

UNIVERSITY	1956	1957	1958
First Year	12	15	15
Second Year	4	3	8
Third Year	2	4	1
Fourth Year	1	1	2
Fifth Year	0	1	1
Teacher Training	18	20	21
Nurse's training	30	29	36[58]

The annual report of 1960–61 reported totals of Indians attending universities at forty-four in 1959, fifty-eight in 1956, and eighty-two in 1961. No statistical breakdown was provided, however.[59]

In 1976, the Indian Affairs department surveyed the participation of Indians in higher education that they were aware of to that point (see Table 2).

TABLE 2: The Indian and Inuit Graduate Register (1934–1976)[60]

GRADUATES BY REGION:

Maritimes	47
Quebec	143
Ontario	128
Manitoba	98
Saskatchewan	93
Alberta	40
British Columbia	75
North West Territories	26
Total Number of Graduates:	**750**

BY DEGREES AWARDED:

Teacher's Certificate	286
Bachelor of Arts	209
Nursing	130
Bachelor of Education	95
Master's degree	45
Bachelor of Science	44
Medical Doctor	11
Law degree	9
PhD	2

BY DECADE OF LAST DEGREE EARNED:

1930s	1
1940s	2
1950s	30
1960s	107
1970–76	610

The types of degrees pursued varied somewhat by region. Indians in the Maritime provinces earned a disproportional number of BA degrees, with twenty-two (47%) of forty-seven of all the degrees earned. Advanced or science-related degrees were most prevalent in Ontario and Quebec. Twenty-four Ontario graduates had earned science-related degrees in areas including chemistry, civil and mining engineering, mathematics, physics, and veterinary science. Fourteen graduates in Quebec had earned science-related degrees. Together, these two provinces accounted for 86% of the science graduates. Ontario also had 71 (55%) of the 130 nursing degrees. As well, seven of the eleven medical degrees were in Ontario. Teachers' degrees or certificates constituted 51% of all graduate listings. In Manitoba, seventy-one (72%) of ninety-eight graduates were in the education field.

A total of ninety-three individuals in Saskatchewan had obtained higher education over the years since 1944. The largest group were the fifty-six teachers mostly holding the "Standard A" designation through the Indian Teacher Education Program at the University of Saskatchewan. Another eleven Indian students completed the Certificate of Social Work program in 1976 through the University of Regina in cooperation with the Saskatchewan Indian Cultural College. While Alberta had a relatively smaller number of degrees, there was a disproportionate number of nurses (nine) and lawyers (two). The types of degrees earned in British Columbia were evenly distributed over various areas. In the Northwest Territories, twenty-four of the twenty-six graduates had obtained teachers' certificates.[61] The differences in the types and numbers of degrees reflected regional variations in educational advancement. In eastern Canada, where the period of contact had been far greater, there was more need of science and professional degrees, to provide nurses, for example, for a hospital that existed on the Six Nations Reserve.

Chapter 3

Increasing First Nations Participation in Higher Education

THE ASSIMILATION THREAT POSED by Trudeau's 1969 Indian policy galvanized Indians into organizing politically and proposing alternative visions of their future. The National Indian Brotherhood, formed in 1970, put forward its policy proposal of Indian Control of Indian Education, which was later adopted by the federal government in February 1973.[1] Indians were keen to pursue political activity and were assisted in this endeavour by funding from the federal government, which wanted the Indians to be able to articulate their policy positions. The inclusion of Indian rights to unfettered access to post-secondary education became a test of the effectiveness of the committee. During this time, the formalization of a post-secondary assistance program to address group rather than individual needs led to a rapid increase in the numbers of Indian students entering universities. The previous program of scholarships for Indian university students had been grafted on to vocational training funding, which was not intended to cover higher education.

General distrust of government by Indians in the period immediately following the issuance of the 1969 Indian policy meant that discussions of policy changes were strained. The Department of Indian Affairs wanted to develop programs in the area of comprehensive claims, devolution of powers to Indian bands, and *Indian Act* revision.[2] To break through distrust and to establish a new process, the department proposed a multi-level approach involving joint committees at the federal Cabinet, bureaucratic, and provincial levels. However, Indian leaders hesitated to participate when it could not be guaranteed that the process would be anything more than advisory.[3]

In a presentation to the Standing Committee on Indian Affairs, Minister Jean Chretien stated that the department would examine six areas in which Indian Affairs would respond to the National Indian Brotherhood's *Indian Control of Indian Education*, including increasing the participation of Indians in universities:

a) involvement of Indians in school management;
b) consultation regarding provincial involvement in Indian education;
c) development of cultural-education centres;
d) development of curriculum;
e) instruction in native languages; and
f) participation of Indians in universities.[4]

In the legal arena, the 1973 Supreme Court's Calder decision, which led to the recognition of Aboriginal rights, was another momentous development. Although the Nisga'a lost the case on a technicality at the Supreme Court in 1972, the substance of the legal arguments was enough to convince Prime Minister Trudeau, a lawyer himself, that the concept of Aboriginal rights had legitimacy. By opening the door to Aboriginal rights, the government cleared the way for policy changes such as Aboriginal comprehensive claims.[5]

Other court decisions also helped shape the face of Indian policy. The 1970 Drybones case in the Supreme Court caused the erasure of the *Indian Act* clause prohibiting Indian alcohol consumption on the basis that such a ban violated the *Bill of Rights*.[6] The Lavell case in 1973 argued that the *Indian Act* discriminated on the basis of sex because Indian women lost Indian status when marrying a non-Indian. The Supreme Court appeared poised to rule that the relevant provisions of the *Indian Act* would have to be struck down. However, Aboriginal political groups objected that such a decision could jeopardize their interests and that any changes should be made by Parliament. The court decided not to force the issue, and Lavell lost the case.[7]

—————•◦•—————

Meanwhile, unrest among Native youth influenced by the Red Power Movement led to militancy at Anishnabe Park in Kenora and during the Native Caravan Trek to Ottawa in 1974, where an RCMP tactical squad forcibly dispersed demonstrators. The caravan had planned to present its main demand that "the hereditary and treaty rights of all Native Peoples in Canada must be recognized and confirmed in the Constitution of Canada."[8] By this time, however, the Royal Canadian Mounted Police perceived the American Indian Movement (AIM), often called in Canada "Red Power," as a threat to national security.[9]

Following the confrontation with Indian militants on September 30, 1974, Indian Affairs Minister Judd Buchanan convened a meeting between the National Indian Brotherhood Executive Council and a group of Cabinet ministers. At the October 9, 1974, meeting, it was agreed that the group would meet once or twice a year as a Special Cabinet Committee to review Indian issues. In a report to the House of Commons, Buchanan described the committee as "a forerunner of future consultations at the ministerial level with the executive of the National Indian Brotherhood." He also reassured Parliament that the *Indian Act* revisions remained the main focus of government.[10]

At the April 14, 1975, meeting of the Special Cabinet Committee, the NIB agreed to a more gradual approach to *Indian Act* revisions. It was also agreed that no changes to the *Act* would be introduced to Parliament without first having been agreed to by the Special Committee.[11] It was this type of understanding that led Indian participants to believe that such a committee was not just consultative, but had real bargaining power.

A discussion paper from the Indian Claims Commission on the committee clearly did not contain that point of view, however. It left no doubt where the real power lay: "final decisions could only be made by Cabinet" and that it seemed reasonable to "exclude from its mandate actual negotiations."[12]

The Parliament Hill confrontation of 1974, with RCMP involvement, highlighted the urgency for a new consultative process with the Indians and led to the creation of the Joint Cabinet/National Indian Brotherhood Committee (JNCC), replacing the Special Committee, later in 1975. This arrangement satisfied Indian concerns that the consultation process be at a high enough political level.[13] In addition, prominent Indian leaders such as Harold Cardinal and Ahab Spence were appointed to senior Indian Affairs administrative positions. These developments were accompanied by a Cabinet document entitled *New Federal Government-Indian Relationship,* which appeared to suggest a new approach.[14] In February 1976, the federal Cabinet formally approved the Joint Indian Brotherhood/Cabinet Committee and agreed on a membership of eight Cabinet ministers and thirteen members of the NIB Executive Council. Working under the committee would be a subcommittee charged with examining issues related to the *Indian Act* and Indian rights in more detail. The group was also to conduct further Indian consultations. According to historian Sally Weaver, the subcommittee itself was to be the "political decision-making forum of the Joint Committee."[15]

It was agreed that education would be the first item of discussion by the committee. The National Indian Brotherhood took the position that two principles must be included. First, the government must accept responsibility for funding all aspects of education of Indians, including college and university education. Second, ongoing funding would be provided to bands as they endeavoured to develop higher education initiatives to meet their needs. The NIB would interpret the committee's response to these proposals as a critical test of the process, which had now dragged into its fourth year.[16]

At the June 27, 1977, JNCC meeting, NIB President Noel Starblanket requested a "substantive response" to the education proposals. The Department of Indian Affair's response was that the potential of expanded band powers in a revised *Indian Act* should be examined first. This was a departure from its earlier position that making sweeping changes should wait until later and, as well, the JNCC had not been given a mandate to discuss *Indian Act* changes. Starblanket cautioned: "We went to work in good faith.... I fear that if we allow ourselves to get into discussions on Band powers then we have to get into the whole gamut."[17] In the NIB's view, this was simply an attempt by the government to avoid making any major concessions.

One of the areas that the Department of Indian Affairs had been working on was amendments to the *Indian Act* that would reflect changes that would satisfy Indian concerns. Revisions to the *Act* were already being contemplated and, in April 1969, the department had conducted a series of national Indian consultations. At those consultations, a key Indian demand was recognition of Indian treaty rights.[18] However, the release of the 1969 Indian Policy, which advocated complete abolition of the *Indian Act,* only added further confusion and volatility to attempts to resolve *Indian Act* issues.

Following the federal government's retraction of the 1969 policy, *Indian Act* revision consultations resumed in 1973. Several Indian organizations had begun study of the *Act* and, in March 1974, the National Indian Brotherhood proposed that the *Act* be radically changed. Alberta Indian Leader Harold Cardinal described it as "a lock, stock and barrel revision of the entire Act."[19] Indian Affairs Minister Chretien preferred to take a more gradual approach, however.[20]

By August of 1974, the National Indian Brotherhood proposals had been submitted to the new minister, Judd Buchanan. These proposals focussed on: a) recognition of enforceable Indian treaty rights; b) legislation that would meet Indian rather than government priorities; and c) measures to promote community development.

In terms of education, the proposals included a section termed "The "Education Right of the Mature Indian." This section addressed the fact that no provisions existed in the *Indian Act* for education beyond the age of sixteen. The proposal defined "Mature Indian" as "those who are fifteen years of age or older and called for adult education funding to be statutory rather than discretionary, and to be available to all without regard to cost."[21] Such funding would cover all costs related to higher education for Indian students, and there would be no limit placed on the number of students who could access the funding.

At the next Joint Committee meeting of July 11, 1977, two Cabinet ministers raised the issue of consulting with provinces on the question of off-reserve Indians. The Brotherhood responded that Indian education was a federal responsibility and that such consultations were unnecessary. This difference of position contributed to widening the gulf between the two sides. It was agreed to refer these questions to the JNCC subcommittee.[22] The subcommittee narrowed the main concern of the federal government down to the amount of funding that would be required if it were to assume total responsibility for Indian education, including off-reserve and post-secondary education. Initial estimates placed the annual cost at close to $500 million.[23]

The issue of consultation remained unresolved by the December 12, 1977, meeting of the Joint Committee. Federal representatives also declared they were not prepared to accept the NIB proposals for education, as it did not seem a proper option when free access to adult post-secondary education was not available to all Canadians. The Brotherhood interpreted this response as government rejection of its treaty obligations.[24] In taking this position, the NIB argued that the federal government was reneging on its acceptance of the Indian Control of Indian Education policy, which included the following statement:

> We must, therefore reclaim our right to direct the education of our children. Based on two education principles recognized in Canadian society: *Parental Responsibility* and *Local Control of Education,* Indian parents seek participation and partnership with the Federal Government, whose legal responsibility for Indian education is set by the treaties and the *Indian Act.* While we assert that only Indian people can develop a suitable philosophy of education based on Indian values adapted to modern living, **we also strongly maintain that it is the financial responsibility of the Federal Government to provide education of all types and all levels to all status Indian people, whether living on or off reserves** [emphasis added].[25]

By 1978, however, the National Indian Brotherhood, under Noel Starblanket, claimed that the chiefs' advice about including post-secondary education in the *Indian Act* was being ignored and that the government was not being forthright. The Brotherhood had believed that the JNCC forum would be one of "nation to nation" negotiation. Trudeau, however, insisted that the Joint Committee would be for high-level policy consultation only, and would not make binding commitments.[26] As a result, Starblanket decided to withdraw the NIB from the Joint Committee, and relations with the federal government became strained. In many ways, however, it was the impasse over funding Indian higher education as a right, and the belief by the NIB that the Joint Committee was ineffective, that doomed it to failure.[27]

A new and more fundamental debate on Aboriginal constitutional issues was looming. In July 1977, the National Indian Brotherhood had made its first request that Indians be involved in constitutional discussions and that Indian rights be "entrenched in any new or varied Constitution of Canada."[28] In a presentation to a House of Commons-Senate Committee in August 1978, the Brotherhood pointed to the patriation of the constitution as an opportunity to recognize a new relationship with Canada based on recognition of Indian sovereignty.

The main focus of the National Indian Brotherhood remained on issues relating to education. Pressing issues included stopping increasing provincial encroachment in Indian education, providing training to enable Indians to take over operation of their schools, and improving curricula to be more relevant to Indians. The Brotherhood, however, also supported the funding of cultural/educational centres with the understanding that "all decisions regarding their evolution be the sole prerogative of the Indian people." Finally, the Brotherhood also supported increased and unfettered access to funding for Indians to enter university, regardless of whether they were beneficiaries of treaties.[29]

One of the most innovative adult education initiatives adopted by the federal government was cultural/educational centres as proposed in the *Indian Control of Indian Education* document. In July 1971, the Cabinet Committee on Social Policy responded by endorsing the funding of such centres for people of Indian ancestry.[30] The concept of such a centre had been originally articulated in the Indian Association of Alberta's *Citizens Plus* counter-proposal to the 1969 Indian policy. One of the main aims of the cultural/educational centres was "to make the process of education meaningful and relevant to the Indian himself, and by doing so, to stimulate a new sense of awareness and self-reliance among native peoples."[31]

The concept of the centres was to provide a means to allow the Indian people to play "a vital role ... in cultural, social and economic development." According to Harold Cardinal, one of the main proponents of the idea, such centres could "look at all facets of adult education and vocational training, curriculum development, experimental kindergarten, primary and secondary schools, with a view that this system would then tie-in with the post-secondary system of the province."[32]

Indian Affairs Minister Jean Chretien described his perception of their purpose: "I see the centres as places and programs in which the cultural heritage of native people will be restored, strengthened, and transmitted both to native people and to the total Canadian society. These centres can also be a resource for new educational probes to make education for native people more relevant."[33]

The federal Cabinet approved a $42 million program for Native cultural centres on July 29, 1971. The Indian Affairs and Secretary of State departments would jointly establish a five-year renewable funding program, with $2 million available in 1971–72 and $10 million in each subsequent year. Eighty percent of the funding was to come from Indian Affairs.[34]

Funding had been approved for a total of nine centres by the end of 1972. By 1973, Indian Affairs had assumed the major role of administering the program, but funding for the program had fallen from $10 to $8 million annually. At the end of the initial five-year period in 1976, Cabinet approved an extension of the program for one year in order to complete a review. However, the program budget also was immediately reduced to $5 million.

In 1978, Evalucan of Calgary, a private consulting company, was contracted by Indian Affairs to evaluate the Cultural/Educational Centres Program. Fifty-one centres were operating, the majority with budgets of under $100,000.[35] The evaluation was guardedly positive, noting, in particular, progress made in the development of Indian curriculum. Some of the deficiencies discovered during the evaluation included a lack of government clarity about the mandate of the centres, as well as confusion over administrative control between the two government departments involved. The evaluation also noted the lack of consultations with Indians when the program was developed, despite such requests by the National Indian Brotherhood.[36] When the program was extended, it included provision for the centres themselves to play a more important advisory role, with the prospect of eventually taking over complete control of the program.[37]

A report by the Aboriginal Institute of Canada was more critical of the way in which the cultural educational centres had been established. It claimed that the Department of Indian Affairs had not been supportive of the concept of the centres to begin with, instead preferring to place its faith in integrated education programs that the department believed were beginning to bear fruit. According to the report, "officials in the Department of Indian Affairs waged a constant campaign to abort the cultural education program. They boycotted interdepartmental meetings, revised their decisions agreed upon at previous meetings, and constantly tried to revise program criteria."[38]

The report identified a basic weakness of the program. Indian Affairs had decided to allocate program funds on a per capita basis, based on the Indian population of a province, and, moreover, gave authority to individual bands to decide how the funding should be allocated. This required directors of larger cultural/educational centres to "spend an inordinate amount of time obtaining and retaining support of various Band Councils. The constant threat of the loss of financial support hampered the continuity of the centres and pitted one group of Indians against another for the limited funds." Due to these difficulties, in 1973–74, the Department of Indian Affairs budget for the program fell to $8 million. Any monies not spent by the end of each fiscal year would be returned to the Consolidated Revenue Fund. Due to the poor communications, only 11.6% of the available funding was used in the first year and 39% in the second year was expended. About two-thirds of the original $12 million in funding for the program had lapsed by then.[39]

The department was criticized for its insensitive approach to disbursement of the program's funds. For example, funding secured for the Saskatchewan Indian Cultural College was arbitrarily reduced by $300,000, despite the hefty surplus remaining in the cultural/educational centres' budget. In 1973, the Indian Cultural College had entered into a joint program with the Faculty of Social Work at the University of Regina to train Indian social workers. The staff of the Cultural College shared teaching responsibilities with the Social Work faculty, and students who were enrolled received assistance from the Indian Affairs department to cover tuition and living expenses. The department was accused of slavish adherence to guidelines and disregard of local needs. Another point of dissatisfaction was the requirement that the centres provide quarterly progress reports, as opposed to requirements of similar non-Indian institutions to report on an annual basis only.[40] Such frequent reporting proved both unnecessary and onerous.

———•◦•———

Manitou College was the most ambitious of the cultural/educational centres, and it had secured college-level accreditation in the province of Quebec. According to Gail Valaskakis, one of the founding board members of the college, the impetus for founding the college came from a group in the Montreal area responding to the National Indian Brotherhood initiative called *Indian Control of Indian Education*.[41] The intent to secure a facility for Manitou Community College was conceived in the fall of 1972, when William Craig, Director of the Native North American Studies Institute (NNASI) in Montreal,[42] learned that the former Bomarc missile base in La Macaza, Quebec, approximately 190 kilometres northwest of Montreal, was available for alternate usage.[43]

The former missile base at La Macaza was a sizeable complex built with American funding and consisting of 185 hectares of land and 173 buildings including administrative offices, social centres, school, gymnasium, golf course, store, and 114 housing units. The facility was turned over from National Defence to Indian Affairs on January 11, 1973.[44]

With the support of the Indians of Quebec Association, National Defence was persuaded to have the missile base transferred to Indian Affairs for one dollar for the purpose of establishing an Indian college. Retired Canadian Forces General Jean Allard, who had taken an interest in helping Indians, played a key role by spending a year and a half negotiating for the abandoned Bomarc missile base site. Department officials apparently made these arrangements without a thorough inspection of the site. Funding would be provided through the cultural/educational centres program.[45] Treasury Board noted that the NNASI had conducted a feasibility study of the facility. The study concluded that the facility would be ideal for use as a cultural/educational centre modelled on the Navajo Community College in Arizona.[46]

Renovations to the base began in November 1972, and on July 2, 1973, Manitou Community College opened its doors. The first program offered was the Amerindianization Program, a summer Native teacher-training program operated through the University of Quebec at Chicoutimi. The term "Amerindian" is commonly used in French Canada, and the objective of the Amerindianization Program was to make the curriculum more relevant to the Indians of the province. In September 1973 an English College of General and Vocational Education (CEGEP) program began, accredited through Dawson College in Montreal.[47] A document formalizing the agreements between these institutions was recognized by the Quebec Department of Education, thereby granting Manitou College accreditation of its academic programs.[48] The following September, the French CEGEP program commenced, accredited through Ahuntsic College, also in Montreal. The francophone program in particular was considered to be an important innovation.[49] By the end of the first year, enrolment in all programs had reached approximately 175 students, all of whom were Status Indians, with the exception of a handful of Inuit students. Of the twenty-three teaching staff, twelve were Aboriginal.[50] Once maintenance staff for the facility and administrative staff were included, the overall staff contingent of the college was sixty-five employees. Academic programs at Manitou College included courses in literature, physical education, mathematics, language, history, sociology, philosophy, psychology, biology, fine arts, cinematography, and graphic communications.[51]

The fall 1974 Aboriginal student enrolment stood at only 122 students: 92 anglophone and 30 francophone. Sixty-seven students were from Quebec, forty-three from the Maritimes, ten from Ontario, and two from the rest of Canada.[52] One factor in the enrolment drop had been academic failures from the previous year. The college embarked on a recruitment drive. The six-week summer Amerindianization Program was again held at the college in 1974, with 153 participants.[53] By the spring of 1975, enrolment had climbed to 130. A first group of thirteen students graduated in May.[54]

Proof of the college's success seemed apparent when compared to the record of the 164 Indigenous students enrolled in Quebec universities in 1972.[55] Ninety percent of the students pursuing higher education in Montreal had dropped out or failed, compared to only 26% who dropped out or failed at Manitou College.[56] An assessment by the Union of Nova Scotia Indians in 1974 reported: "they [the students] said the college enabled them to enjoy education, develop their identity and self-confidence. As a result, few dropped out."[57] In 1974, the Inuit Association of Northern Quebec agreed to have their cultural/educational funds given to the college: "These Inuit students expressed satisfaction with the social and living conditions at the college. While at the same time they would, from time to time, go to Montreal to learn to function in the southern world."[58] In the winter of 1974, the Recreation Committee of the Indians of Quebec Association held its first Winter Games at the college, and over 500 youth participated.[59]

In November 1973, early in the college's development, William Craig resigned due to ill health, and George W. Miller was asked to take over as General Director.[60] The college faced two immediate challenges: achieving financial stability and establishing academic credibility. The quarterly cultural education grant in the winter of 1974, which included tuitions but not student housing payments of $10,000, was $226,000, a shortfall when compared to monthly operating expenses of $246,000. When combined with initial start-up costs, such as for furnishing the 110 housing units, the college's first forecast deficit stood at $168,700.[61]

The financial report for the year August 20, 1973 to August 23, 1974, noted that federal funds to Manitou College included $826,000 cultural/educational grants and a one-time $500,000 capital grant.[62] The report noted that, in response to the less than expected revenues, a series of cutbacks, including layoffs and returning goods, was instituted. Thirty-four employees had been laid off, including six professors.[63] The shortage of funds prevented the college from expanding its library collection of 3000 books.[64] These measures still resulted in a higher than anticipated debt of $225,677 by March 31, 1974. By the fall of 1974, the college was attempting to negotiate a more favourable lease agreement with the Department of Indian Affairs.[65]

In the early stages, the college experienced difficulty with cost recording and controls. However, a progress report indicated that implementation of the auditor's recommendations had greatly improved the accuracy of financial accounting. In his closing remarks in the progress report to August 15, 1974, the General Director stated: "Our financial position has improved considerably since November 1973 so that the College can positively hope that it is becoming a permanent institution."[66]

The progress report also indicated that the Quebec Department of Education would provide the college with $348,000 in student enrolment grants in the upcoming fiscal year.[67] Such payments were made on the basis of Manitou College's academic affiliation with the English-language-based Dawson College and the French-language-based Ahuntsic College, and were not construed as a provincial commitment to Indian post-secondary education. The college's financial comptroller ended the report on an optimistic note for the upcoming year: "Our deficit projection really stands at only $33,000. This is, in my opinion, a remarkable performance by a first time Indian College."[68]

In May 1974, the college received permission from the Quebec Department of Education to create a new series of classes with Amerindian content, which would become part of the recognized bank of courses in the CEGEP system. Negotiations were also being conducted to transfer the University of Quebec (Chicoutimi) teacher-training program to the college.

With no other Indian-controlled programs to compare it to, Manitou Community College was an experimental model.[69]

Until this time, the Native North American Studies Institute had administered the operations of the college. In August 1974, a new board structure for the college was developed, which included one representative from each of the Quebec Indigenous groups: Abenaki, Algonkian, Atihkomewk, Cree, Huron, Inuit, Micmac, Mohawk, Montagnais, and Naskapi.[70]

A recruitment program was initiated to raise the profile of the institution and attract students. As recruiters travelled throughout southern Ontario and northern Quebec, they found that school counsellors and Indian Affairs officials had minimal information regarding the college. Many believed it was primarily an upgrading and vocational institution, and were not aware it offered college-level courses. There were also many questions about college facilities and operations. Some officials expressed concern about the distance to the college. The Director of Education of the Union of Ontario Indians indicated that some Indian Affairs offices were refusing to fund students to attend the college because of uncertainty about the program.[71]

In an article circulated among college staff, a faculty member wrote her thoughts about the college's growing pains and the stakes involved:

> Manitou Community College is a baby that is striving for survival.... Outsiders—both Native and non-Native—are watching this institute with critical eyes.... If this institute fails, then we will be held responsible forever, and the Bureau of Indian Affairs will continually say to other Native people who will try again to do what is being tried here that the project was tried once and failed.[72]

By 1975, circumstances seemed to turn against the college. The OPEC oil cutbacks caused oil prices to escalate, presenting a significant heating cost increase and worsening the college's financial situation. The Indian Affairs department became more demanding of the college's financial reporting and regularly withheld its quarterly payments. Paycheques for staff began to be delayed. Rumours began to circulate that Manitou College might be shut down.

On January 28, 1976, Indian Affairs indicated that the Cultural/Educational Program's initial five-year term would end on March 31, 1976, and that the program would undergo a review.[73] By February 3, 1976, National Indian Brotherhood President George Manuel expressed concerns that the Department of Indian Affairs was making statements casting doubt on the future of Manitou College. "Because of the tensions which you have created in this situation, I would suggest that you could relieve this anxiety by meeting with the Indians of Quebec who are concerned ... the people have lost confidence in the Departmental staff who have been trying to relay the department's policy in this matter."[74]

On February 19, 1976, a letter signed by sixty-five staff and students of Manitou College was forwarded to the Minister of Indian Affairs. The letter, authored by Professor Claude Rabeau, stated insightfully that

> the Amerindian population has never benefited from appropriate and competent educational institutions where they can feel fully accepted and not discriminated against. Manitou College is the only one in eastern Canada that is able to become an institution totally adapted to the needs and legitimate aspirations of the Amerindian population. I have heard that the principal motive for closing Manitou College would be for financial reasons. I believe that this reason would be very short-sighted.... It would be premature to kill in its infancy, an experience so full of promise.[75]

The letter concluded by asking the minister to meet with college staff to explain his position.

The college began receiving Indian political support. The Traditional Hereditary Chiefs of Oka sent a Band Council Resolution dated February 20, 1976, in which they stated their "faith in the ideal and objectives of Manitou College ... we strongly insist that the survival of this college be assured.... The withdrawal of necessary funds or a relocalization will be interpreted as the funeral of our cultures."[76]

College Director Miller was facing pressure from non-Aboriginal employees as well. Responding to a request from Local 10294 of the Public Service Alliance of Canada for an immediate 15% salary increase, the director pointed out that the college had not received an operating increase during its three years of existence. He noted that a study had indicated that in order to fully maintain college facilities and programs, it should be receiving an annual grant of $1.9 million. Its current budget was only $865,000. He noted that Canada was giving billions of dollars to the Montreal Olympics and ruefully stated, "When we try to lift ourselves up by the bootstraps and restore our pride and position in our own country by establishing such institutions as Manitou College, we must beg for every cent and put up with harassment, petty obstacles put in our way by petty non-Native bureaucrats in the very department that is mandated to look after the welfare and affairs of Indians."[77]

In the meantime, a controversy was brewing. Senator Guy Williams wrote a letter to Minister Buchanan, asking him to investigate media reports of an outbreak of venereal disease at Manitou College, and a report that sixty individuals had refused to be medically examined. He suggested that operations at the college be suspended until such time as the health situation was addressed.[78] In his response, Minister Buchanan noted that a report in the *Globe and Mail* about the outbreak had little basis in fact: "It would appear that the information given by the person involved constituted his own personal opinion and it was particularly unfortunate that his comments were published in the press without any attempt to check upon their correctness."[79] Nevertheless, the minister noted that these reports had been met with alarm by the students' parents and home communities.

The original college Board of Governors had been replaced in August 1974 by a board representing the First Nations, to whom the funding had originally been given. Some of these bands had begun to consider that they might prefer to have these funds expended in their own communities, a situation that threatened the funding base of the college. A review by Indian Affairs of the financial situation of the college noted that with a reduction in the amount of funding given by the Cultural/Educational Program, including the withdrawal of their portion of funds by some bands, the college would receive only 64% of its anticipated revenue. The official declared: "The gravity of the situation which they [the financial statements] portray makes it imperative that the future of this college be taken under very serious consideration without further delay ... it is ridiculous to look on this as a viable operation when it is in such a state of insolvency."[80]

Matters came to a head at a meeting of the Manitou College Board of Governors in December of 1976. The financial situation of the college revealed growing anticipated deficits. Two officials of Indian Affairs in Ottawa, representing the Cultural Education and Development divisions of the department, were present. They reiterated their support for the cultural/educational centres program, which now had fifty-three centres operating across Canada. They noted, however, that the global cultural education budget had been reduced from $7 million to $5 million. They concluded that the most urgent problem facing Manitou College was its deficit, and recommended that "drastic measures" be taken.

When board members were asked for responses, the student representative stated, "It would be a crime to close the college." Responses from some of the chiefs on the board revealed, however, that a political rift had already occurred. Chief Andrew Delisle, speaking on behalf of the Indians of Quebec Association, stated, "The chiefs expressed their concern that the [cultural education] monies stay at the Band level" to be spent on local initiatives.[81] A resolution was passed "that the activities at the present site of the College be temporarily suspended; the students be oriented towards other institutions for January 1977," and that a Management Committee be set up to study new structures. The motion was carried with five in favour and three abstentions.[82]

Details of the Manitou College board meeting were relayed in a briefing to the Minister of Indian Affairs, and the department was notified that the Indians of Quebec Association had no further use for the facility. The briefing noted that "the Department feels that any criticism levelled at activities within the college or decisions by the college should be addressed to the responsible authorities, and dealt with as an internal matter." In doing so, the department would deflect its role in the decision, pointing to the Indian organizations instead.[83]

A further briefing to the Minister of Indian Affairs on December 10, 1976, reported that arrangements had been made with the Quebec Justice Department to provide additional officers on standby to assist the two already on-site at the college if necessary in the event that there were protests or other resistance to closing the institution.[84]

Once the department had obtained the desired decision, events moved forward quickly. In late December, when most staff and students were away for Christmas holidays, the college's Board of Directors suddenly shut down the institution. The closing was a devastating experience for those who helped establish the institution or believed strongly in their work there. The local police had been put on alert in the event of trouble and a sit-in of teachers and students at the college later that month had to be dispersed. The facility has since been turned over to the Quebec government and now serves as a medium security prison, which undoubtedly counts many Aboriginals among its numbers. According to Gail Valaskakis, one of the major problems was that Indian Affairs did not have the vision to see the long-term benefits of an institution such as Manitou College.[85]

Funding for Manitou College came to represent about 17% of the department's reduced budget of $5 million. Had the original Indian Affairs budget of $10 million been adhered to when the college started, the college's budget would have represented only 8%. Valaskakis believes that the department could have funded the college as an experimental project apart from the funding earmarked for the various First Nations of Quebec. Although the college had relatively low enrolments, it was retaining a much higher number of students than provincial universities, and was beginning to gain regional and national recognition for its innovative programming offered in cooperation with the Quebec's CEGEP college system. Unfortunately, however, Indian Affairs had not been ready to embrace the notion of First Nations-controlled higher education.

Perhaps the greatest legacy of the college was the students it nurtured. Among the graduates, for example, one became a lawyer, another a CBC producer, yet another a freelance reporter, and another an internationally recognized artist. Others worked as researchers for the Royal Commission on Aboriginal Peoples. It is highly doubtful these students would have been able to reach these goals had they not attended the college. Many other successes might have been possible had Manitou College been allowed to continue its mission.

In 1968–69, 250 Indian post-secondary students who were experiencing difficulty obtaining funding support under mainstream training programs were assisted through Indian Affairs. This motivated the department to begin looking internally for sources of program funding. The 1972 *Indian Control of Indian Education* document went further, focussing on guaranteed funding support for all Indians wishing to attend universities, and on seeking "representation on the governing bodies of institutions of higher education."[86] Minister of Indian Affairs Jean Chretien acknowledged the aspirations of Indian people for higher education, and he credited increased enrolments to university admission arrangements for mature students and to the department's financial support. The latter was identified as the key element. However, Indian Affairs showed no interest in developing Indian-controlled higher education programs or institutions.[87]

In 1975 Indian Affairs unilaterally began developing the "E-12" guidelines, regulations that prescribed how funding was to be administered for Indian post-secondary students. Assistance was based on federal Manpower training program allowance rates. Although Indian organizations protested the lack of consultation about the guidelines, the criticism did lead to modifications, including the dropping of provisions requiring contributions by students, the meeting of performance standards, and the increasing of maximum allowable time to complete a program.[88] The National Indian Brotherhood initiated a consultation with Indian post-secondary students and released its findings in 1976, but Indian Affairs rejected these recommendations as too costly. While accepting the purpose of the E-12 guidelines, the Brotherhood rejected any restrictions on the principle that there should be unfettered access.

In 1977 the rapid increase in the number of Status Indians and Inuit enrolling in colleges and universities led Indian Affairs to create the Post-Secondary Education Assistance Program (PSEAP). The objectives of PSEAP were to encourage such participation and to fund the maximum number of students who qualified for entrance.[89] The University Entrance and College Entrance Preparation Program were added in 1983 to assist students who were not fully qualified to complete those requirements but could be funded at the same level as fully qualified students.[90]

Indian students had followed these developments with great interest. At a 1978 National Indian Education Conference in Ottawa, post-secondary students formed the National Steering Committee of Indian Students to continue to pursue changes. On December 15, 1978, the committee met with the Minister of Indian Affairs to request that student funding be put on a more stable footing and that university education be recognized as a general right under the education provisions of the treaties.[91] The minister rejected that position, and although he promised to work with the NIB on the issue, no further action resulted.[92] Despite the opposition, the numbers of Indians participating in higher education increased from over 800 in 1972–73 to 2606 by 1978–79. Overall funding for post-secondary training grew, reaching $7.1 million by 1974–75 and $10.3 million by 1978–79.[93]

By 1978, the department finalized its PSEAP guidelines. The program supplied what was, in essence, a non-limited budget and virtually any Indian accepted into university could receive funding. With this program, Indian enrolments at universities mushroomed from 60 in 1961 to 13,196 by 1987. Unfettered access to universities would not be easy to sustain and Indian Affairs warned that cutbacks were necessary.[94]

By 1982–83, student enrolment had grown to 6500 with an annual cost of $34.1 million. After a survey of students, administrators, and band representatives, the Indian and Northern Affairs Evaluation Branch report concluded that the PSEAP was a success and had satisfactorily met all its objectives, among which was to achieve a post-secondary participation rate comparable to mainstream society.[95] Completion rates, however, were still significantly below the national norm for a variety of reasons, including students' inadequate educational preparation and difficulties in adapting to mainstream society. The report asserted that employment levels among successful Indian graduates approached that of the national norm. It noted that about 50% of graduates worked directly for Indian bands and organizations, and that many of the remainder worked indirectly through schools or government agencies.[96] No major revisions or additions to funding were recommended, but increased counselling and tutoring support, greater Indian involvement in determining priority areas for training, and transferring program administration from Indian Affairs to bands and tribal councils were suggested to improve the program. The report also proposed funding a "native center" at institutions that had high Indian student enrolments.[97]

While university-based Native Studies programs have played a significant role in Indian higher education, they are not funded by Indian Affairs, nor are they Aboriginal-controlled. Despite the fact that universities are major beneficiaries by virtue of the First Nations students who are funded to attend their institutions, universities have not been significantly involved in the development of Aboriginal higher education policy. A 1987 article on the development of Indian/Native Studies in Canada noted that the initial motives for establishing Native Studies related primarily to a desire to study the changing situations of Native peoples in Canada:

> The historical roots of Native Studies, therefore, lie in universities' attempts to rectify past failures by establishing programs which would accurately reflect the native experience in Canada ... there was a recognition of the need to correct the distortions imposed by neo colonial European view of Canadian history and culture ... another influence on the emergence of Native Studies has been the recognition that educational institutions ought to become more instrumental in equalizing Native opportunity for participation in society.[98]

Pressure to address Native Studies within the university was generally led by non-Aboriginal faculty who were interested in the area (such as anthropologists), as well as by the few Native students entering the system. Native Studies programs often entailed pooling existing faculty resources from various disciplines, and non-Natives in classes often outnumbered Native students. Native Studies programs such as the first one created at Trent University in 1969 assumed that "Native Studies would develop as an academic discipline consistent with the established norms of the University, stimulating the intellectual growth of students and undertaking research in accord with the accepted rules of academic inquiry," while at the same time being "consistent with and a reflection of native culture."[99]

Dr. Joseph Couture, Native Studies Department Head at Trent University, recognized the difficulties in this process, including overcoming an "absolutist" Eurocentric view of knowledge, the lack of an "established canon" in Native Studies, and the challenges of validating traditional knowledge provided by oral histories and elders.[100] Some academics, such as American Indian professor Dr. Elizabeth Cook-Lynn, have remained highly critical of much of the scholarship that has emerged in universities: "in spite of the burgeoning body of work by Native writers, the greatest body of acceptable telling of the Indian story is still in the hands of non-Natives.... [T]hey reflect little or no defense of treaty-protected reservation land bases and homelands to indigenes."[101]

Native teacher-education programs at universities, of which there were about twenty in 1986, have made a unique contribution to the development of Indian education policy. Professionals in the field have had the opportunity to work directly with First Nations parents in articulating changes they believe were required.[102] One of the issues these teacher trainees had to address was the importance of First Nations education in bringing about relevant social change in Aboriginal communities. Such a development was controversial, not just because Indian education had historically been focussed on assimilation, but also because it represented taking back power over their communities.[103] Now that the policy direction for education is in support of Aboriginal self-determination, new challenges have arisen. There is recognition that education for self-determination is a complex process, but necessary for the development of healthy communities.[104]

In 1961, Father Andre Renaud initiated a summer course on Indian schooling to help Indian teachers to instill cultural pride in their children for their own culture, and he also helped the Federation of Saskatchewan Indians to obtain facilities at the University of Saskatchewan to house its Saskatchewan Indian Cultural College.[105] In another initiative at the university, the Faculty of Law developed the Native Law Program because "Native people do not have ... any meaningful representation in the ranks of the legal profession."[106] It began as a summer program modelled after one at the University of New Mexico, designed to give students the study and research skills necessary for them to compete at the same level as non-Native lawyers. Ten of the initial fourteen students went on to law school.

A Department of Native Studies was established at the University of Saskatchewan in 1983. A 1987 survey of 6119 students in arts and science at that university indicated that only sixty-seven identified themselves as being of Native ancestry. Faculty members who were concerned about the admission cut-off grade for students of 73% lobbied for an Affirmative Action Program, which was granted in time for the 1987–88 academic year.[107] From 1987 to 1990, fifty-two Native students were admitted under the exemption, but of those, only twenty-seven were still active in 1990, indicating an ongoing problem of Aboriginal student retention. However, the total number of arts and science students identifying themselves as having Aboriginal ancestry had grown to 220. Although the Aboriginal students "are treated just like any other student," by 1990 the college was implementing special orientations and tutoring services, and was making the Native Studies Elders Program more accessible.[108]

A number of departments with full majors in Native Studies have arisen since the establishment of Trent University's program. Brandon University founded the second Native Studies program and the first in western Canada in 1975, with focus on literature and archaeology. The University of Manitoba also established a Native Studies department in 1975, and many researchers took advantage of their proximity to the Hudson's Bay Archives to produce new studies on Aboriginal people and the fur trade. Other Native Studies departments exist at the University of Alberta, University of Lethbridge, University of Saskatchewan, University of Sudbury, and St. Thomas University (see Appendix C).[109]

Currently, there are efforts to "indigenize the academy" at universities such as the University of Saskatchewan, where "experience has also revealed deeper assumptions and practices which, in effect, reaffirm Eurocentric and colonial encounters in the name of excellence, integration, and modernity. Aboriginal peoples' achievements, knowledge, histories and perspectives have been ignored, rejected, suppressed, marginalized or under-utilized."[110] Measures include focussing on recognition of Indigenous values and worldviews, and incorporating these in teaching and research. The extent to which indigenization of large mainstream universities is possible depends on whether Aboriginal people are granted a significant presence on the institution's governance system as well as on whether significant funding is provided to programs for Indigenous peoples.

A comparative study of four Native Studies programs noted that an institution controlled by First Nations, such as the Saskatchewan Indian Federated College, had a unique advantage in being positioned to respond to the needs of Aboriginal communities. A common challenge faced by Native Studies programs has been the acceptance by the university communities of culturally relevant and practically oriented courses. It noted that "First Nations involvement has signaled a shift in the acceptance of cooperative curriculum development [between universities and First Nations] as a model versus an exception."[111]

The organization that has come closest to representing the interests of Native Studies programs is the Canadian Indigenous/Native Studies Association (CINSA, formerly the Canadian Indian/Native Studies Association) founded in 1983. The objectives of the organization, adopted in 1984, included to:

a) foster the exploration, articulation, and application of research and education grounded in Indian/Native philosophies and concepts;

b) encourage and support the development of Indian/Native Studies at Canadian universities and colleges, and the professional development of persons engaged in such programs;

c) foster communication between Indian/Native Studies departments and programs in Canada through the holding of meetings, conferences and symposia;

d) promote research and publication of Indian/Native studies;

e) liaise with local, national and local educational associations and Indian/Native communities; and

f) promote the immediate and long-range concerns of Indian/Native studies departments and programs.[112]

An effort by the association in 1988 to propose an area of strategic grant funding was initially rejected by the Social Sciences and Humanities Research Council of Canada (SSHRC) panel of adjudicators on the basis that CINSA represented "but a small proportion of all of the eligible scholars in Canada" and had a "too focused orientation to the historical studies of treaties."[113] In response, CINSA President Blair Stonechild refuted the lack of national representation in its membership, pointing out that the 103 members came from universities in British Columbia, Alberta, Saskatchewan, Manitoba, Ontario, Quebec, and the Maritimes. This response resulted in the awarding of a $15,000 grant to identify the needs in Indian/Native Studies Research, and resulted in a short-lived funding program. The episode revealed the difficulties of making new inroads in the entrenched system of established academic disciplines at SSHRC, where the validity of Indigenous knowledge or the value of Aboriginal community-based research methodologies had not yet been recognized.

The goals of First Nations higher education institutions appear to vary qualitatively in terms of the emphasis on "pure" or "unbiased research" by mainstream universities as opposed to the emphasis on community ties and relevance. As distinguished American Indian scholar Vine Deloria notes, "The first point which we must consider in reviewing any set of essays that pretend to offer an objective view regarding Indian affairs is that there never has been an objective point of view regarding Indians and there never will be."[114] Moreover, First Nations-controlled institutions are generally funded tenuously at a level below that of mainstream public institutions, hence it is difficult for them to maintain equivalent levels of research or to attract the most qualified scholars.

The 1996 report of the Royal Commission on Aboriginal Peoples was critical of the roles played by universities. It noted that universities tended to be assimilative: "Everyone is expected to fit." The commission recognized that universities are attempting to integrate Aboriginal requirements by creating programs such as Native Studies that incorporate Indigenous content. The report observed that the student completion rates are unacceptably low, often because Aboriginal students felt "isolated in a hostile environment where professors and students express racist attitudes and opinions."[115] The report urged mainstream universities to recognize that "the accommodation of Aboriginal culture and identity should be regarded as a core responsibility of public institutions," and that there be "commitment to Aboriginal programs and support services by integrating costs into operational budgets."[116] The report also suggested that aggressive pursuit of funding by universities seeking to pursue their own agendas and priorities in Aboriginal education could impinge on First Nations efforts to gain control over these important functions.

Chapter 4

Student Demands and Funding Caps

ABORIGINAL AND TREATY RIGHTS became entrenched in the Canadian constitution after a great deal of political struggle. Such developments created more public awareness of Aboriginal rights and interests and opened the door for new government policy initiatives. However, an issue of fundamental importance to First Nations, the inherent right of sovereignty, remained unresolved over the course of the constitutional talks between 1983 and 1987. Attempts by the Nielsen Task Force to cut back on government funding created tension towards, and mistrust of, the Mulroney government, which was in the midst of Aboriginal constitutional negotiations.

The issue of access to higher education rights became a controversial policy issue by 1987 when the federal government denied that higher education was an Indian right and attempted to cap higher education funding as part of a general initiative to cut government expenses. This action came during a period when the interest of First Nations students in attending university was growing at a fast pace, and institutions such as the Saskatchewan Indian Federated College were expanding. First Nations students staged a series of national protests to fight this turn in government policy.

In 1984, near the beginning of the Aboriginal constitutional talks, the federal government had given funding to the Assembly of First Nations to conduct a major national consultation on education. This study, coordinated by the National Indian Education Forum (NIEF), issued its findings in 1988 in the report *Tradition and Education: Towards a Vision of Our Future.*[1] This document strongly advocated the sovereign right of First Nations to control all aspects of their education, and emphasized the importance of higher education in achieving self-determination.

One of the main motives for Pierre Trudeau's foray onto national politics had been to bring Canada into a form of renewed federalism, a model Trudeau believed ideal for a vast, diverse country such as Canada. In the process, he would also stifle the forces of separatism by excluding the *deux nations* concept from the constitution. The main challenge would be to find a Canadian-made amending formula to replace the role played by the British Parliament in the *British North America Act.* In addition, a charter of rights would be added to the new constitution to protect civil, bilingual, and minority rights. The election of René Lévesque and his separatist Parti Québécois in 1976 added more urgency to the situation.[2]

An initial constitutional proposal in 1977 failed when anglophone premiers failed to win the trust of Quebec's Levesque. Aboriginal organizations, on the other hand, had been totally left out of what was seen as a purely federal-provincial process. Aboriginal leaders, realizing the constitution's importance for the recognition of Indian self-determination, insisted they be included when the constitutional talks resumed in 1979. However, they were offered observer status, which was unacceptable, so the leaders opted to boycott the talks instead.[3]

The National Indian Brotherhood decided to carry out an extensive lobby campaign in Britain in an attempt to have Queen Elizabeth II honour the Indian treaties signed on behalf of the Crown. Appeals through the office of Canada's governor general had been fruitless, and a reply from Her Majesty, which stated "the Queen fully recognizes the great importance attached to discussions which have begun," persuaded the Indians that the Queen was being misled, as no such discussions had ever occurred.[4] In 1979, a delegation of 300 chiefs and elders, organized by Clive Linklater of the

National Indian Brotherhood, travelled to London. On July 2, 1979, the British media gave massive coverage to the All-Canada Chiefs Assembly.[5] The next day, the chiefs met with representatives of the House of Lords and House of Commons and, the day after that, took a petition to Buckingham Palace that asked the Queen to honour the litany of Royal decrees issued regarding First Nations. While they failed to get an audience with the Queen, who had been advised by Ottawa not to become involved, the palace agreed to study the issues.

When some British politicians began to investigate the matter, Canada's treatment of its Aboriginal people threatened to become an embarrassing obstacle to patriating the constitution to Canada. In the face of this publicity, the Liberal government agreed to allow a limited form of Aboriginal participation in future constitutional discussions. However, the loss of the election to Joe Clark's Conservatives in 1979 brought a brief hiatus to the constitutional process.[6]

Trudeau returned to power unexpectedly the following year in time to face a Quebec referendum. The separatists' loss of the referendum motivated Trudeau to make another effort at resolving the constitutional issue. In preparation for continuation of the constitutional process, the National Indian Brotherhood had transformed itself into the Assembly of First Nations (AFN), reflecting the Indians' view of themselves as nations negotiating with Canada.[7] Continued "stonewalling" in Ottawa caused the Indian lobbyists to intensify their efforts to oppose the resolution to patriate the constitution, which was due to arrive at the British Parliament in November 1980. Included in their strategy was an appeal to a human rights tribunal in Holland, an act that resulted in a condemnation of Canada.[8]

As a result of the lobby, the Canadian government extended its constitutional hearings for six weeks in order to hear Aboriginal concerns. In February 1981, Prime Minister Trudeau announced the inclusion in the proposed constitution of section 35: "The Aboriginal and treaty rights of the Aboriginal peoples of Canada are hereby recognized and affirmed."[9] The term "Aboriginal" included Indians, Inuit, and Métis, a victory for the latter group, as it was the first time they were recognized at the federal constitutional level.[10]

This important advance was soon undone, however. In November 1981, Trudeau made another effort to get the premiers to agree on an amending formula. At this time, the premiers, with the exception of Levesque, in a late-night session dubbed the "kitchen accord," agreed to Trudeau's amending formula with some changes. Prairie premiers, alarmed at the rising expectations of Indigenous groups, and realizing that substantial powers and resources could be at stake, had taken a firm stand against entrenchment of Aboriginal rights or self-government. References to Aboriginal rights were struck from the final draft of the constitution.[11]

Public announcements by both the Canadian and British governments that the constitution was ready to be "repatriated" led to a desperate round of last-minute First Nations lobbying. Federation of Saskatchewan Indians leader Sol Sanderson interrupted Indian Affairs Minister Chretien's press conference in London to present a Declaration of the First Nations. He also challenged in the British courts the contention that the British Crown no longer had any obligations to Indians.[12] The case was rejected, but Justice Lord Denning declared that Canada had an obligation to uphold the treaties signed with the Indians. On December 23, 1981, the *Canada Bill* received first reading in the British House of Commons. Indians disrupted the second reading of the bill, causing shocking news stories in Britain and Canada.[13]

Continued, persistent, and sometimes frantic lobbying, combined with the support of the women's lobby, succeeded in embedding section 35 in the *Constitution Act.* This time, however, the word "existing" was inserted before the term "Aboriginal rights" in an attempt to limit its scope. The *Constitution Act.* was finally given Royal assent on March 29, 1982.[14]

The First Nations also managed to secure reassurances in section 25 of the *Canadian Charter of Rights and Freedoms* that nothing in the constitution would

> abrogate or derogate from any Aboriginal, treaty or other rights or freedoms that pertain to the Aboriginal peoples of Canada including (a) any rights or freedoms that have been recognized by the Royal Proclamation of 1763; and (b) any rights or freedoms that have been acquired by the Aboriginal peoples of Canada by way of land claims settlement.[15]

The inclusion of the word "existing" in section 35 had been a deliberate attempt to limit Aboriginal gains through the constitutional process. There was no clear consensus about what these "existing" Aboriginal rights were. It would, therefore, become necessary to identify these rights in a series of constitutional conferences, held in 1983, 1984, 1985, and 1987.

———•◦•———

The central focus of debate during the constitutional conferences on Aboriginal peoples had been the issue of sovereignty and the Aboriginal right to have control over all aspects of their lives. During this period there were also demands for the recognition of First Nations higher education rights. When Minister of Indian Affairs Bill McKnight unilaterally imposed a cap of $93.7 million on Indian post-secondary funding in June 1987, it was seen as a major setback. Instead of unlimited access, Indian students would now be eligible to receive funding on a priority basis only.

There was speculation that the cutbacks had really originated with the 1985 Nielsen Task Force, which had advocated dropping Indian Affairs programs that were not statutory requirements. In an approach reminiscent of the 1969 Indian Policy, the task force argued that federal funding of Indian programs had failed to address Indian needs, and that much of this funding should either be discontinued or transferred to the provinces.[16] Cutting back spending was one of the top priorities of the Mulroney government, and Deputy Prime Minister Erik Nielsen had been given broad powers to review government programs. In Nielsen's view, the issue was simply one of streamlining government through the elimination of program duplication. The task force submitted a 523-page document that proposed radical changes. Forty percent of Aboriginal funding was deemed to be "for what would normally be provincial and municipal services" and 35% was seen as "discretionary, based on incremental social policy decisions."[17] The real implications for First Nations policy were, in fact, dramatic. Many of the programs would be turned over to provincial and municipal governments, and the Department of Indian Affairs would become redundant. All these changes would occur without the input of Native people.[18]

The task force also argued that the provinces already received transfer payments for higher education, including that for Indians, and that the Indian Affairs funding amounted to a duplication of services. On another issue, concern was raised that promises to increase post-secondary funding to cover the 50,000 individuals whose Indian status had been reinstated under Bill C-31 had not been fulfilled.[19] Nielsen's recommendations were in direct contradiction to statements made by Prime Minister Brian Mulroney, during the 1985 constitutional conference, that Canada's special relationship with its Aboriginal peoples could not be changed without consultation, and that it would not only be protected but even strengthened. While Mulroney denied that Nielsen's task force recommendations constituted government policy towards Aboriginal people, the credibility of the Conservative government had been irretrievably shattered. Although no cutbacks to First Nations programs occurred in the 1986 federal budget, the fear was that any future funding was, in fact, "capped."[20]

In the fall of 1986, Indian Affairs arbitrarily imposed a cut-off date of November 1, after which no further students would be funded for the remainder of the fiscal year. This action prompted letters of concern from students, Members of Parliament, and the Assembly of First Nations. In his letter, Keith Penner, MP for Cochrane-Superior, noted that this sudden and unannounced action had "disrupted the lives and plans of many people and has caused unnecessary anguish, frustration and anger."[21] Further, stated Penner, the move was in conflict with recent commitments by the minister to "shift decision-making to where it belongs—with Indian communities ... and establish a greater degree of stability and self-reliance."

The Canadian Federation of Students weighed in by noting that eighty students had been denied access to the Saskatchewan Indian Federated College because of the cut-off.[22] The Ontario Regional Chief for the Assembly of First Nations charged: "Once again, you and your department have violated the commitment made by Prime Minister Mulroney in 1985 when he assured us of full and open consultation on all issues affecting First Nations."[23]

On March 19, 1987, Minister of Indian Affairs Bill McKnight responded to concerns from the Standing Committee on Indian Affairs regarding the cut-off with the commitment that should further changes to post-secondary funding occur, "Every effort will be made to make that [decision] in time that it will not affect the education plans of Indian students."[24] In an April 10, 1987, briefing to McKnight, the details of a strategy to revise the E-12 guidelines began to emerge. The cutbacks that would be imposed were:

a) a student would have to be resident in Canada for 12 months prior to application;

b) student grants would be awarded in place of multi-allowances, thereby simplifying funding;

c) elimination of the provision granting graduate students the equivalent of half of their salary, if they had taken a leave of absence from work;

d) reduction of the funding assistance period from a maximum of 96 to a maximum of 48 months;

e) adult upgrading education outside of university and college upgrading was no longer eligible; and

f) students would be funded on a priority basis and appeals would not be allowed on the basis of non-availability of funding.

Previous funding arrangements that remained unchanged included:

a) financial assistance would be available to Status Indians and Inuit, with allowances increasing according to number of dependents;

b) assistance would include living allowance, tuition, and books and supplies;

c) student grants would not have to be repaid; and

d) travel costs would be provided for students and their dependents who needed to relocate in order to obtain post-secondary training.[25]

Program costs would not be allowed to exceed the allocated budget of $93.7 million, in effect capping the funding. Additional funding to cover students who had been reinstated to Indian status would be sought from Bill C-31 implementation provisions. It recommended that in order to allow for adequate consultation, program commencement should be April 1, 1988.[26]

In early May 1987, the department sent to First Nations chiefs a letter announcing "immediate interim changes" to post-secondary funding. The letter referred to the one-year residency requirement in Canada, elimination of a half-salary option for funding graduate students, prohibiting appeals based upon a lack of funding, etc., but made no mention of plans to limit student funding. The letter claimed that program funding had increased ten-fold from $8 million to $81 million over the previous decade, and concluded by stating that the department would be seeking discussions regarding further changes to the program.[27]

McKnight invited First Nations to participate in consultations to improve the Post-Secondary Education Assistance Program. Among the objectives of the review would be to see how Indian groups could take more responsibility for managing the program while making it more cost-effective and relevant to achieving the goals of Indian self-determination. It was intended to be "demand-based" rather than an unlimited provision of funding. Indian reaction to the proposal was that higher education was a right, and that Indian Affairs was abandoning its responsibilities.

By the fall of 1987, an estimated 300 Saskatchewan Indian students had been denied funding.[28] The following year, the number of denied students had grown to about 1000. By the following year, Indian students had become politically active. On September 15, 1988, a national series of protests were staged. In Saskatoon, 100 students picketed the Saskatoon office of Indian Affairs. A statement issued by the Federation of Saskatchewan Indian Nations warned: "Canada faces the option of investing resources of Indian education now or continuing to pay the penalty for its shortsighted-ness in years to come. Canada's expense will be in costs associated with welfare, prisons, foster care and other symptoms of social disorder."[29]

John Parry, MP for Kenora-Rainy River, was among the first to level criticism at the announcement. He deplored the absence of consultation with Aboriginal people, and contended that with an average 24.5% annual increase in demand for funding by First Nations students, the "cap" placed on funding was ill-advised. Parry wrote that while the Nielsen Task Force advocated ending the "double funding" of Aboriginal higher education by federal and provincial governments, it did not propose cutting back First Nations post-secondary funding. In fact, it appeared to acknowledge the importance of providing such opportunities, Parry claimed.[30] In his response to Parry, McKnight denied any intention to cap post-secondary funding. He claimed that post-secondary funding would continue to be a priority for Indian Affairs, and that the findings of the Nielsen Task Force supported the department's actions.

By October 1987, the government was facing demonstrations over its lack of consultation regarding changes to Indian post-secondary funding, including the still unofficial "capping" of funding. In fact, although the funding for 1987–88 had been frozen at $93.7 million, no decision had been made regarding funding for subsequent years. Minister McKnight made that point in response to an inquiry from the Canadian Association of University Teachers: "I must first tell you that the level of funding has not been capped. Our budget for this program was increased by 15% over last year [for the 1988–89 fiscal year] and I expect that next year's budget [for the 1989–90 fiscal year] will show an increase from that of the current year."[31]

In January 1988, the department developed a "press line" regarding the funding controversy. In assessing the situation, the department recognized that "sit-ins and demonstrations drew the attention of the public-at-large to the dissatisfaction of certain Indians with the program."[32] The press line pointed out that the auditor general had criticized Indian Affairs in 1986 and 1988 for the lack of data on educational achievement, and that the department was simply trying to do a better job by being more accountable for post-secondary expenditures. Canada, it said, was "head and shoulders above other countries" in such a program, including the United States, where a similar number of Indian students received only a quarter of the funding.[33]

The auditor general's report for 1986 had noted that resistance from First Nations political organizations had hampered Indian Affair's efforts to institute guidelines for the administration of education funding. Nevertheless, the department was still accountable to Parliament and had to arrive at better reporting systems.[34] The criticisms regarding post-secondary funding were more specifically laid out in the auditor general's 1988 report: "Monitoring practices varied from region to region, ranging from periodic visits to band offices in Alberta and British Columbia to virtually no visits in Manitoba."[35] In seventy individual student files that were examined, "we found many errors. There were inaccurate payments, funding for ineligible students and courses, and lack of documentation to support the payment of shelter and child care allowances."[36] The report noted the lack of a legislative basis for the program, and that "DIAND [Indian Affairs department] has not clearly defined whether bands and tribal councils, in taking charge of PSEAP for their members, are assuming a management role (with the authority to change the rules) or only an administrative role.... [T]he Department must provide bands with a clear and consistent policy framework." The report concluded that Indian Affairs needed to "ensure consistency with program policies" and "maintain relevant, basic program information."[37]

By March 30, 1988, Indian Affairs Minister McKnight announced that consultations with First Nations would take place between May to December 1988, and that the new policy would be implemented by April 1, 1989. He also promised that the new policy would include greater local control: "It is my intention to include in the revised policy the provision for local administrations to develop their own operating guidelines. This is consistent with Indian Control of Indian Education."[38] The National Indian Brotherhood had argued for control over such programs during the Joint Cabinet/ National Indian Brotherhood meetings of the mid-1970s, and that funding be formalized as a statutory obligation.

In order to provide context to Aboriginal constitutional discussions, the federal government had provided funding to the Assembly of First Nations (AFN) in 1984 to undertake a major consultation and discussion regarding Indian education. This funding had resulted in the AFN's establishment of the National Indian Education Forum (NIEF) under the direction of Dr. Mike Charleston. The forum's report, *Tradition and Education: Towards a Vision of Our Future*, released in August 1988, began with a "Declaration of First Nations Jurisdiction over Education." The declaration proclaimed that First Nations were sovereign entities with the inherent right to control their own educational destiny, including control over post-secondary education. The report called on the government to provide adequate levels of funding on a non-discretionary basis. On the specific issues of jurisdiction and rights over post-secondary education, the report stated:

> Post-secondary education is essential to all First Nations activities that share the objective of self-determination.... Trained First Nations pro-fessionals play a crucial role in the development and implementation of strategies contributing to self-determination. First Nations are

requesting direct participation in decisions affecting post-secondary education for First Nations students.... *The data gathered and analyzed from the First Nations by all three research programs strongly affirmed that post-secondary education is an Aboriginal right of First Nations* [emphasis added].[39]

The report also addressed issues of development and management of post-secondary education:

In keeping with self-determination initiatives, all of the reports also pointed out the need for more community-based opportunities for post-secondary training where experience can be more practical and students are not required to relocate. The design of effective post-secondary level management is a rapidly growing concern to individual First Nations, in terms of technological development, as well as the transition to local jurisdiction.... *A current priority in education for Canada's First Nations is to establish Constitutional guarantees for adequate financial resourcing of post-secondary education....* First Nations must also ensure that quality education facilities exist that are on par with and are better than provincial or territorial standards [emphasis added]."[40]

The greatest individual concern, raised by 72% of respondents, was that living allowances, which had not increased since 1982, were inadequate, especially for students with dependents. Eliminating daycare expenses and special allowances for travel would make their circumstances more difficult. Interestingly, the report noted, "Married students, older students and women have higher post-secondary and occupational success rates than others."[41] Disparity in access to education still existed, compared with the general population, as a 1987 Statistics Canada report found that "Indians are only one-third as likely to be enrolled in university programs."[42]

Another area of concern noted by the forum was that it appeared that Indians, whose status had been newly reinstated by Bill C-31, would now be added to the pool of individuals requiring funding, without an accompanying budget increase. This would run counter to promises by former Minister of Indian Affairs David Crombie that reinstatements under Bill C-31 would not detract financially from existing programs.

The NIEF report noted that it cost $10,000 to put an Indian through a year of university, compared to up to $56,000 per year to house them in a high-security prison. As part of the report, the Association of Universities and Colleges of Canada analyzed comparisons between the PSEAP and the Commonwealth Programs for Developing Countries. The association found that grants provided to Commonwealth students totalled $18,000 to $20,000 per year. Moreover, those students were allowed more flexibility in choosing which programs they wished to attend, and spouses could earn more money before being disqualified as dependents.[43]

The students objected to the policy by holding rallies, the first in Ottawa on October 21, 1987. In June 1988 Indian Affairs undertook to consult with bands on their policy, mainly by mailing out questionnaires. By late 1988, Indian student organizations were complaining about the inadequacies of the consultation process.

Demonstrations over post-secondary changes resurfaced in the fall of 1988, with a protest in Regina in early September and another in Thunder Bay in October. The department did not resist attempts to occupy its offices, and in one case provided the services of a nurse to monitor the condition of five fasting students.[44] Additional demonstrations were being planned for Toronto and Ottawa. In its press line, the department contended the students were wrongly assuming that the proposals had already become policy. It described its program, which spent 63% on non-tuition financial support for students, as generous, and claimed that relatively few students had been denied support.[45]

While the Assembly of First Nations supported a demonstration by activists planned for June 12, 1989 in Ottawa, it had not mounted an effective political campaign against the cuts. Assembly of First Nations National Chief Phil Fontaine was preoccupied with a much larger issue, that of defeating the Meech Lake Accord. Instead, the AFN seemed to be relying on the public sympathy that student protests would generate. However, this strategy was not successful. In a document marked "secret," the Deputy Minister of Indian Affairs was advised: "Given the relative lack of media interest in the demonstration on May 13 ... our approach should be low-key." Other reasons for the low-key approach included what were perceived as successes in communicating the new policy to the Standing Committee on Aboriginal Affairs, and the conclusion of an agreement on devolving post-secondary funding with the Federation of Saskatchewan Indian Nations.[46]

When new Minister of Indian Affairs Pierre Cadieux officially announced the revised policy in February 1989, a backlash was not unexpected. Students organized the "National Day of Protest" on April 1, 1989. Demonstrations occurred in every province, Indian Affairs offices were occupied, and some students went on a thirty-six-day hunger strike. In some cases, criminal charges of "public mischief" were laid.[47]

In March 1989, Minister Cadieux announced that after consultations with students and with over 500 bands, organizations, and associations, a new program called the Post-Secondary Student Support Program (PSSSP) had been created. He noted that the department's funding of Indian post-secondary students had grown from approximately 3500 in 1977–78 to 15,000 in 1988–89 and that costs had correspondingly risen from $9 million to $130 million, an amount in excess of the 1987 funding cap. The minister had determined that costs could not continue to escalate and "a small number of students will temporarily have to seek those sources of support available to all other Canadians." Cadieux asserted that he thought the program, which was not generally available to Canadians, was "generous and fair" and was "unparalleled anywhere in the world." Finally, he clarified the federal government's position on Indian higher education by rejecting outright the notion that such funding was a treaty right: "For the government, the position is crystal clear ... treaty references to education do not include post-secondary education.... The government has funded this special program to ensure that a significant number of Indian students attain university-level qualifications."[48]

The Standing Committee on Aboriginal Affairs report released in June 1989, in the midst of the Aboriginal higher education controversy, appeared to suggest that some resolution to the issue of funding entitlement might be possible. The report claimed that in 1979, at the urging of the National Indian Brotherhood, funding for the Post-Secondary Education Assistance Program became non-discretionary, which meant that funds could no longer be transferred out of the program arbitrarily during the funding year.[49] As well, Indian Affairs Minister William McKnight had initiated a consultation process on Indian higher education in 1988. However, many Indian groups regarded the consultation as inadequate since it involved mainly a canvassing of opinions and did not include any real dialogue about decisions.[50]

In his 1989 presentation to the standing committee, new Indian Affairs Minister Cadieux had reiterated the government's rationale for the post-secondary funding cutbacks:

> Everyone knows that there are not unlimited funds for any form of government expenditure. Nevertheless, the Indian and Inuit Post-Secondary Assistance Program grew from $4.2 million to $130 million in 13 years. Furthermore, the number of students over that 13-year period has grown from 2,500 to some 15,000 students now. In other words, the student population has increased more than seven times while the budget has increased more than 30 times its original amount.[51]

When questioned by the committee about whether higher education was a treaty right, Cadieux clarified his earlier position: "Since the actual words in the treaties do not refer to higher forms of education, I simply cannot base a post-secondary education program on treaty rights. Additionally, not all Indians are protected by treaties and not all treaties mention education." When challenged on the narrowness of this claim, he conceded, "Obviously, only the courts can legally interpret the treaties."[52] As well, the committee noted the 1987–88 Auditor General's Report's concern that there was "lack of a clear legislative mandate for funding or delivering [Indian] post-secondary assistance."[53] In its recommendations, the committee stated: "The Committee is clearly not in a position to decide the substantive legal issue of whether or not post-secondary education is a treaty right. The Committee strongly recommends that a forum be created to resolve this fundamental disagreement."[54] This comment was a reflection of the fact that lower court decisions, such as *Greyeyes v. The Queen,*[55] had rendered the opinion that Indian post-secondary funding flowed from the treaties. However, the issue had never been referred to higher courts. While the federal government denied that any specific references to higher education existed in the treaties, nevertheless, the existence of its extensive programs implied some sort of obligation.

On July 5, 1989, the Assembly of First Nations attempted to capitalize on the Senate report by passing a resolution that moved, among other things, that "the Chiefs in Assembly demand that the Minister of Indian Affairs and Northern Development, Pierre Cadieux, retract his claim that post-secondary education is not a treaty right," and further, that the Assembly "strike a negotiation committee to establish a treaty and Aboriginal rights process with respect to education."[56]

The student protests over Cadieux's policy resulted in consultative meetings between Indian Affairs and Indian representatives on August 25, 1989. The department agreed to soften the policy in a number of areas, including funding provisions, extent of assistance, and appeals. However, the funding cap on the renamed Post-Secondary Student Support Program would remain at $130 million until 1991, when an additional $320 million was to be added over five years.

In regard to the issue of recognizing post-secondary education as a treaty right, the National Indian Education Forum, which had overseen the consultations that had resulted in the *Tradition and Education* report, took exception to the statements made by Minister Cadieux. The NIEF criticized such statements as being narrow and legalistic, and not honouring the spirit and intent of the treaties with respect to the right to education. It noted that decisions of the Supreme Court such as *Nowegijik v. the Queen* held that "Treaties and statutes relating to Indians should not be literally construed and doubtful expressions resolved in favor of the Indians." The report called for Cadieux to retract his statements, and further contended that the courts or political agreements, and not simply Indian Affairs, should be the final arbitrator. The NIEF called for a forum to be created in which this disagreement with the federal government could be resolved.[57] The NIEF noted that recent controversies over the PSSSP had "contributed greatly to discouraging First Nations students from ever applying," as some had concluded from media reports that no funding would be available for them. Cadieux was urged to issue a statement immediately confirming that all qualified students would be accepted, a recommendation the minister ignored.[58]

In August 1989 in Saskatchewan, the Federation of Saskatchewan Indians and Indian Affairs established a Policy Review and Change Working Group. In its preliminary recommendations regarding PSSSP, the group recommended that no Treaty/Status Indians should be denied access to funding as a result of the policy. It noted that students were often faced with high costs due to relocation to urban centres, and recommended that some accommodation be made to cover relocation costs. It noted that "42% of children in subsidized care [in Saskatchewan] are Treaty/Status Indians" and it recommended that costs to cover daycare be reinstated.[59] The working group also recommended deletion of the "single student living with an employed parent" category, as they thought that single students should not be penalized for choosing to remain in the security of the parental home.

The Saskatchewan Indian Federated College (SIFC) registered its criticism of the new PSSSP, stating that the new guidelines did not respect the recognition of the Aboriginal right to education despite the fact that treaties were now enshrined in the constitution. The college criticized the cutbacks in light of the fact that demand for education was increasing. It also noted that the cutbacks would discourage Indian students from outside the province attending SIFC's unique programs, due to the emphasis on cost reduction. Finally, it called upon the federal government to support the college's development as a centre of excellence.[60]

In September 1989, Cadieux announced further modifications to the PSSSP to be implemented as a result of recent consultations, including more flexibility in cases such as emergency travel, confirmation of support for graduate level studies, and a better appeals process. The minister noted:

> I am very much aware of the profound conviction of Indian people that post-secondary education is a treaty right. That is why I have indicated to the Standing Committee, and in my discussions with chiefs and leaders in your communities, that I am prepared to discuss and consider any new information on treaty rights and post-secondary education in a separate forum where a full discussion of this important issue can take place.[61]

In November 1989, the Evaluation Directorate of Indian Affairs released its assessment of the old PSEAP program. It concluded that PSEAP had succeeded in significantly increasing Indian post-secondary participation from 2500 in 1975-76 to 15,000 by 1988-89, with numbers almost doubling over the last five years (see Table 3). It noted, however, that the 1988 auditor general's report identified the program's management information as being inadequate.[62] The evaluation included 387 telephone surveys, combined with other data. The directorate noted that there had been some opposition to the study, including bands who refused to provide information, and the cancellation of a focus group "due to the lack of cooperation among students at several institutions."[63] In the directorate's opinion, however, this opposition did not bias the study's results.

TABLE 3: Students Utilizing the Post-Secondary Education Assistance Program (PSEAP) 1975-1990

YEAR	NUMBER OF FULL- AND PART-TIME STUDENTS	PERCENT INCREASE
1975-76	2500	7
1976-77	2684	7
1977-78	3599	34
1978-79	4148	15
1979-80	4502	11
1980-81	4999	9
1981-82	5467	25
1982-83	6810	23
1983-84	8062	18
1984-85	8617	7
1985-86	11170*	30
1986-87	13196*	18
1987-88	14242*	8
1988-89	15572*	9
1989-90	18535*	16

*Figures for these years include the number of Bill C-31 students.[64]

Of the students in PSEAP, only about one-quarter were registered in university, the rest being mainly community college students pursuing one- or two-year programs. The study also noted that 69% of the students were female, one-third were married, and the overall average student age was 28.4 years.[65] While the PSEAP had been successful in increasing participation rates, completion rates and associated costs were seen as unacceptable. In a typical year, less than 15% of the students had completed their year's program. Those who successfully completed tended to be enrolled in shorter community college programs of one or two years' duration, and tended to be married. Major reasons identified for failure were family responsibilities and the lack of adequate finances. Significantly, three-quarters of those who withdrew indicated a desire to return to studies in the future.[66]

There was a 76% non-completion rate among students in the social sciences area, the areas in which well over half the students were enrolled. The evaluation determined that PSEAP had not succeeded in increasing participation in science and health-related areas, as only a miniscule 2% of graduates had completed such programs. Finally, there was a high failure rate in the University and College Entrance Preparation (UCEP) program, a situation blamed on a lack of screening and support.[67]

TABLE 4: Students Assisted, Per Student and Total Expenditures, PSEAP, 1981–1989[68]

YEAR	NO. OF STUDENTS	PER STUDENT EXPENDITURES	TOTAL (MILLIONS)
81–82	5469	$4,591	25.1
82–83	6,810	4,860	33.1
83–84	8,062	5,210	42.0
84–85	8,617	6,139	52.9
85–86	11,170	6,347	70.9
86–87	13,196	7,267	95.9
87–88	14,242	7,520	107.1
88–89	15,048	8,054	121.5

On the positive side, the evaluation report noted that 87% of the program's graduates succeeded in finding employment, generally in long-term, meaningful positions. Surprisingly, 92% of the students who withdrew were able to find employment. However, it was also clear that the desire for employment was sometimes a reason for students to withdraw, as the jobs they took tended to be less permanent and not necessarily in their area of studies. Nevertheless, the report concluded that having been involved in PSEAP created positive opportunities for students, especially females, to access employment.[69]

———————

The Saskatchewan Indian Federated College had been originally created in May 1976 as a bold initiative in Indian-controlled post-secondary education. Affiliated with a provincial university, the University of Regina in Saskatchewan, the college has grown from a humble beginning of a dozen students to an institution of over 1600 students and over 2000 graduates. The Department of Indian Studies, considered to be the academic core of the college, has evolved a broad, yet highly articulated, curriculum with an emphasis on research.

The SIFC was created as a result of growing political consciousness, in particular the movement that had begun among the Indian people of Canada in the early 1970s for Indian control of Indian education. Problems of relevance of education coupled with a high dropout rate meant that very few Indian students entered university. For the Federation of Saskatchewan Indian Nations (FSIN), formerly called the Federation of Saskatchewan Indians (FSI), the political organization that represents the seventy-two chiefs and approximately 100,000 First Nations people in Saskatchewan, this meant control not only over primary and secondary education, but also their post-secondary education.[70]

As part of their thrust towards Indian control of Indian education, the FSI in January 1974 had presented a proposal to the University of Saskatchewan for a "setting up of an Indian College in Saskatchewan." The federation, as well as other Indian organizations, was attempting "to make the federal government realize the legitimacy for setting up Indian colleges in the country." It was proposed that an Indian-controlled college would offer Indian Studies courses as well as provide professional education in areas such as teacher education, social work, and administration. However, the University of Saskatchewan, concerned that such an idea was untried and wary that academic quality might be compromised, responded negatively to the proposal.[71] In reaction to a request presented to the Cabinet in 1975 for funding for the proposed Saskatchewan Indian College, Gordon MacMurchy, Minister of Human Resources Development, replied, "The province at present does not fund the college as the policy assumption is that it is totally funded through the federal department." He noted, however, "that the government would certainly be willing to make themselves available to help resolve problems of jurisdiction in the hope of making the federal government accept their responsibility."[72]

In a memo to Saskatchewan Premier Blakeney, MacMurchy reported that Indian Affairs Minister Buchanan was "adopting a hard line on FSI demands."[73] The FSI was also discussing with Premier Blakeney the possibility of streamlining services to Indians under a "One Agency Concept." Such an approach would prevent overlapping and confusion in the delivery of services to Status Indians, both on and off reserves. It was hoped that with provincial support, the federal government would also cooperate.[74]

In early November 1976, Chief Ahenakew expressed to Premier Blakeney appreciation that "the relationship between the Federation of Saskatchewan Indians and the Provincial Government continues to be a co-operative one." In the letter, Ahenakew asked the Blakeney government to accept the concept "that Indian policy is to be developed by Indians with government responding and adjusting to the degree to which it is possible."[75] In order to do that, Ahenakew pointed out resources would be required in order to conduct long-range planning. Blakeney was asked to approve federated status for the new Saskatchewan Indian Federated College and that the province participate in operational funding, along with eventual provincial participation in capital funding.

The Federation of Saskatchewan Indians embarked on creating a series of institutions at the post-secondary level. First Nations elders, including Smith Atimoyoo, Ernest Tootoosis, and Jim Kanipitehew, had identified the need for more culturally and socially relevant programs in history, politics, and philosophy at the university level.[76] They travelled to various First Nations communities to consult and obtain support to establish an institution that would help to train Indian professionals such as teachers, social workers, and administrators.

In 1976, newly appointed university president Dr. Lloyd Barber, who had recently completed a term as federally appointed Indian Claims Commissioner, recognized an opportunity to undertake a new and exciting venture in partnership with the Saskatchewan Indian people. First Nations enrolments at the University of Regina prior to the establishment of the college had never exceeded more than about a half-dozen students out of a university student body of several thousand.[77] At the beginning of his mandate, Barber proposed to the FSI the "federated college model" of higher education delivery.[78] Federated colleges are intended to allow smaller learning environments and are administratively and financially independent, while being academically integrated with the university.[79] The federal Department of Indian Affairs provided core funding, and the college shared SIFC student tuitions, retaining 40% for on campus students, with the university. A provincial grant reflecting the enrolment of non-Aboriginal students in the college rounded out the funding. Many regarded the creation of an Indian-controlled college as a novel experiment, since the institution was being created within a community that had no tradition of university level education, and had very few individuals who possessed university credentials. Under the Federation Agreement, the institution's proposed program was approved by the academic structures of the university and qualified staff were hired in consultation with the administration. The SIFC delivery model became a unique entity in North America in that it was an Indian-controlled college working in academic partnership with a major public university, and no other similar arrangements have been created since.[80]

The Saskatchewan Indian Federated College was eventually incorporated under FSI legislation, the *Saskatchewan Indian Federated College Act*. The college began by offering a degree in Indian Studies in 1976, degrees in Indian Art, then expanded into Indian Languages and Indian Education in 1977, and into Indian Management and Administration in 1978.[81]

In 1976, the FSI had been concerned by a federal "Native Policy" proposal to lump Indian, Métis, and non-status programs under one umbrella. It feared a revival of the 1969 assimilation policy. A "Provincial Native Policy Paper" prepared by the Saskatchewan government appeared to be designed to cooperate with the initiative. When confronted by the FSI, Gordon MacMurchy responded on behalf of Cabinet: "The Federation of Saskatchewan Indians can anticipate the continuing support of our government in its approach to Federal Government-Indian relations." MacMurchy reassured FSI Chief Ahenakew that the paper would be "withdrawn and suspended." Furthermore, he confirmed that the government's approach would be "that your Federation develops policy positions for Indians. Our role as a government is to respond in ways which ... are acceptable to both your Federation and the government." Dick Fedorick was appointed as a liaison person with the federation. In essence, the province had accepted the federation's leading role in Indian policy development.[82]

By the time of the fall FSI annual conference in 1976, David Ahenakew claimed: "We convinced the provincial Government to recognize that education was a treaty right and a federal responsibility." He continued, "We now have a professional college at the University of Regina where Indian Studies will be taught to our students from *our* point of view."[83] Continuing Education Minister Don Faris commended the FSI: "The pattern of good counsel and discussion developed between FSI and this Department has led to history-making improvements in the field of adult education by native people for native people."[84] The provincial government's general policy moved to support FSI positions based on treaties, and this included the federal government's responsibility to provide funding for higher education.

In remarks during a meeting with the premier, Chief Ahenakew stated, "The relationship which is evolving between ourselves and your government is the envy of many Indian Organizations across Canada. They often find that the absence of such a relationship in their own provinces is a critical vacuum in their efforts to secure Indian rights." He also noted that efforts to get the federal government to live up to its responsibilities were "greatly enhanced by an open and co-operative relationship with the provincial government."[85] The federation referred to the college as "a major breakthrough and a significant step forward for Indian education in North America. This is the only place, to the best of our knowledge, where Indians have succeeded in establishing a formalized, equal partnership with a university."[86]

In early 1977, Chief Ahenakew chastised Minister of Indian Affairs Hugh Faulkner for a lack of political will to resolve issues such as funding for the SIFC. He noted how quickly funding could be arranged for projects such as pipelines once the government decided to act. That November, Ahenakew requested a meeting with Faulkner "to resolve the issue of responsibility for funding of the Saskatchewan Indian Federated College." He maintained that "there isn't room for debate" about the Indians' right to education stemming from the treaties, and he asked to discuss a submission to the Treasury Board concerning core funding for the college.[87]

While communication between FSI and the province appeared to be excellent, the same could not be said for the federal government. Provincial Indian Claims Coordinator Rob Milen referred to Faulkner's response to land entitlements as "a tremendous failure to communicate." The federal government appeared to be reneging on promises to place federal Crown lands on the table, and Milen suspected that federal bureaucrats were waiting "to see if a government less sympathetic to the Indian cause is elected."[88]

By October 1977, the province was urging the federal government to "support the post-secondary education of Registered Indians." At the same time, protest was made about an apparent initiative "to shift responsibility for post-secondary education for Registered Indians onto the provinces." In the interim, the province would supply special funding of $100,000 to SIFC for "research and development."[89] In September 1978, the province provided $203,000 in developmental funding to the college on the understanding that operational funding was a federal responsibility. If federal funding was not forthcoming, the province was of the opinion that "the FSI will find it necessary to seriously consider terminating the college's operations."[90]

Later that month in a press release, Faulkner tried to embarrass the Saskatchewan government into accepting full responsibility for the SIFC: "The federal government could not assume continuing financial responsibility for the administration of a college which, as a post-secondary institution, is clearly the responsibility of the provincial government...." The Department of Indian Affairs "has neither the funds nor the authority to establish and operate post-secondary institutions," he continued. He pointed out that the *Established Programs Funding Act* transferred full funding for post-secondary education of all citizens, including Indians, to the provinces. He concluded that provincial failure to fund SIFC amounted to "discriminatory action."[91] Such intergovernmental bickering was extremely disconcerting to those struggling to develop the SIFC during this early period.

Taking advantage of the disagreement, the FSI requested that "approximately 5% [of higher education transfer funds] ... $5,850,000" be turned over to the Federation as the Indian share of higher education funding. The province denied that Indians were included in the census figures used to calculate the funding; Vice-Chief Sol Sanderson noted "somebody is wrong."[92] In December 1979, Sanderson took the position that the province should at least be providing funding for the approximately 20% of non-Indian students attending SIFC.[93] This arrangement would bring additional revenues to SIFC without raising provincial jurisdiction issues.

It would not be until John Munro became Minister of Indian Affairs that the federal government began to deal with the issue of SIFC funding by processing a request for core funding through Cabinet. Factors in this breakthrough were that the provincial government threatened to withdraw funding, Saskatchewan Indian leaders had close political ties with Munro, and the federal government was under intense pressure to tackle First Nations constitutional issues.[94]

In April 1980, MacMurchy informed new FSI Chief Sol Sanderson that Minister of Indian Affairs John Munro was now willing to deal with funding for the SIFC. In July 1981, the Department of Indian Affairs entered into a Memorandum of Agreement on Tuition Services, under which per capita tuition fees for registered Indian students would be provided to the college. It was not until the 1985–86 fiscal year that Cabinet gave Indian Affairs the authority to change funding arrangements to a discretionary operating grant of $3,308,000. Such funding was supplemented by sharing university tuitions with the college. Part of the federal funding understanding at the time was that the Province of Saskatchewan would participate in future core funding arrangements.[95]

The first director of the college, Ida Wasacase, a member of the Ochapowace First Nation and a well-known educator, established an institution that reflected strong control by First Nations, while meeting the academic standards and regulations of the university. She reported to the college Board of Governors, which consisted primarily of chiefs representing ten regions of Saskatchewan, but also included representatives of the University of Saskatchewan, University of Regina, and the federal and Saskatchewan governments. Wasacase's approach emphasized bicultural education, in which the student would learn about, and thus be able to function in, both the Indian and white worlds. For example, while there was to be a department teaching the five Indian languages in Saskatchewan—Cree, Saulteaux, Nakota, Dakota, and Dene—there was also a Department of English.[96]

Reaching First Nations students in their own communities was deemed a priority, and a significant amount of teaching activity occurred in the form of off-campus classes as well as entire degree or certificate programs offered on a one-time basis in First Nations communities. Approximately fifty off-campus classes were offered in various communities across Canada during the 1998 academic year, and the college established campuses in Saskatoon and Prince Albert for the significant First Nations urban student populations in those areas.[97] The college also frequently offered programs on a demand and cost-recovery basis in most of the provinces and territories including British Columbia, Alberta, Manitoba, Ontario, Quebec, Northwest Territories, and the Yukon.

Chapter 5

Gaining Control

THE ASSEMBLY OF FIRST NATIONS' 1988 *Tradition and Education* report, commissioned in connection with Aboriginal constitutional negotiations that began in 1983, espouses a new vision of the empowerment potential of First Nations education. Combined with First Nations' political pressure, the report would lead to a new Indian Affairs higher education policy initiative, the Indian Studies Support Program. This program was designed to increase access to higher education in First Nations communities, to provide support for First Nations-controlled programs, to enhance a few programs in provincial universities, and to fund the Saskatchewan Indian Federated College as a special provision. The new policy was to increase First Nations student participation in higher education and community-based programming. This led to increased interest in the potential, characteristics, and effectiveness of First Nations-controlled post-secondary education.

The 1996 report of the Royal Commission on Aboriginal Peoples (RCAP) strongly endorsed the First Nations' efforts to achieve recognition of Aboriginal sovereignty. Aboriginal organizations viewed Minister of Indian

Affairs Ron Irwin's response to the RCAP report—that the Canadian
government would recognize First Nations' self-government based on
the devolution of municipal-like powers—as inadequate. The Royal
Commission also made recommendations regarding First Nations' control
over higher education funding and establishment of their own institutions,
echoing the recommendations of the *Tradition and Education* report.

———••••———

The Royal Commission has sparked policy debates, mainly in academic
circles, about the balance between Aboriginal sovereignty and the extent to
which Aboriginal people are a part of Canadian society. Issues of pragmatism
versus ideology are prominent in this debate. The work of three scholars,
Menno Boldt, Alan Cairns, and Tom Flanagan, typifies the different
approaches. Menno Boldt, in his *Surviving as Indians: The Challenge of
Self-Government,* focusses mainly on pragmatic issues such as what are
the fundamental goals of current Indian leadership. He wonders whether
current First Nations leadership is falling into the trap of becoming the elites
of their societies, co-opted by the mainstream agenda and ultimately not
meeting the needs of their own communities. The author also questions
whether Indians should be mainly focussed on cultural adaptation and only
secondarily on finding ways to preserve the positive aspects of culture
within their emerging societies.[1]

Political scientist Alan Cairns takes a more balanced approach,
criticizing the approach of Aboriginal leadership who espouse a parallelist
view of history, the idea of independent societies going down the path of
history side by side but having few meaningful ties. He describes parallelist
thinking as the opposite extreme from assimilationist policy, and being an
equally misguided approach. Interestingly, Cairns was part of the team who
produced the Hawthorn Report in 1963, which originally coined the term
"citizens plus" in reference to the special status of Canada's Indians. Cairn's
principal point is that all people in Canada are citizens of the nation, and, in
order to develop a healthy society that engenders mutual respect, it is best
for all people to be interdependent and interconnected.[2] Boldt and Cairns

both point out that urban-based Aboriginal populations tend to be younger and better educated, and hold more potential for having the critical mass to bring about sorely needed change. However, while such policy commentators do offer insights, they often fail to address the full range of Aboriginal responses and proposed solutions to policy issues, particularly at the local community level.

Tom Flanagan, the most ideological and conservative of the policy commentators, contends that the fundamental principles underpinning Aboriginal rights and self-government are misguided because First Peoples were originally primitive and did not possess the intellectual, social, and political sophistication to which they now aspire. Flanagan criticizes First Nations' sovereignty, which he interprets as "ultimate control or independence,"[3] as not possible for First Nations for a variety of reasons, including the lack of cultural experience in managing the affairs of the modern state. He also cites the lack of sufficient population, land base, and resources, and denies the legitimacy of Aboriginal rights, upon which any such arrangements for recognizing sovereignty might rest.[4] He points to other pragmatic problems, claiming that the call by the Royal Commission on Aboriginal Peoples for "state to state" relations between Canada and approximately seventy First Nations would be unwieldy, inefficient, and unproductive. He criticizes the proposed RCAP solution as unrealistic and unwise, and contends that, as a primarily First Nations-territory approach, it ignores the reality that over half the Aboriginal people now reside off-reserve.[5] Unfortunately, Flanagan's xenophobic views cut off any reasonable discussion of alternatives for the future.

The fight for Aboriginal rights caught the imagination of many Canadians during the constitutional debates of the 1980s, and public support for its inclusion in the constitution was high. Given this background, the First Ministers believed that inclusion of further Aboriginal demands in the constitution might be possible. The Charlottetown Accord offered the First Nations what they had been seeking: recognition of the inherent right of self-government.

> The Constitution should be amended to recognize that the Aboriginal peoples of Canada have the inherent right of self-government within

Canada.... The recognition of the inherent right of self-government should be interpreted in light of the recognition of Aboriginal governments as one of three orders of government in Canada.[6]

However, in a national referendum, the general Canadian citizenry rejected the Accord. Ironically, the majority of Aboriginal people also voted against it, concerned that the implications of the proposals were not clear enough. It may not have been the Aboriginal inherent right to self-government that was so controversial, as this enjoyed substantial public support, but rather the section that accorded Quebec a perpetual guarantee of 25% of the seats in the House of Commons, something that smacked of another elitist deal. The demise of the Charlottetown Accord has left the issue of Aboriginal self-government in a vacuum.

The idea of First Nations self-government was not new. The key recommendation of the 1983 *Report of the Special Committee on Indian Self-Government* (Penner Report) was "that the federal government establish a new relationship with Indian First Nations and that the essential element of this recommendation be recognition of Indian self-government. The Committee recommends that the right of Indian peoples to self-government be explicitly stated and entrenched in the Constitution of Canada." The report contended that additional measures should also be implemented, including provision of sufficient funding to properly deliver programs, as well as the transfer of additional lands and resources to First Nations.[7]

In a similar vein, the RCAP stated

that Aboriginal Peoples have a right to fashion their own destiny and control their own governments, lands and resources. They constitute nations, with an inherent right of self-government.... All of our recommendations for governance, treaty processes, and lands and governance are based on the nation as the basic political unit of Aboriginal peoples. Only nations have a right of self-determination.[8]

The Royal Commission also emphasized the creation of viable institutions: "Only at the national level will Aboriginal people have the numbers necessary to exercise a broad governance mandate and to supply a large pool of expertise. At the national level they can develop institutions that are stable and independent of personality."[9]

Alan Cairns and the Penner Report both support the concept of self-determination—"freedom to chose one's own fate or course of action without compulsion"—and contend that a viable measure of self-government, "controlling or ruling oneself,"[10] is not feasible for First Nations to pursue independently, but is possible with the active cooperation and support of the Canadian state.[11]

———•◦•———

The RCAP, the most expensive Royal Commission to that time, had conducted extensive research on the histories and issues of Aboriginal peoples. While Aboriginal peoples hoped that the commission's report, released in 1996, would set the road map for further changes, the federal government appeared to have shelved its fundamental recommendations; for example, recognizing the inherent sovereignty of First Nations and entering into new relationships on that basis.

Minister of Indian Affairs Ron Irwin's August 16, 1995, release of the *Federal Policy Guide on Aboriginal Self-Government* indicated the federal government would take a different approach from that of the Royal Commission.[12] Irwin's proposed amendments to the *Indian Act* would result only in the devolution of municipal-like powers, a strategy that had already been rejected by First Nations.[13] The recognition of this form of self-government would not be based upon the principle of inherent sovereignty. First Nations leaders launched angry but futile protests in the lead-up to the June 1997 federal election.[14]

In the area of Indian higher education, the commission recognized its primacy in terms of achieving the goals of Aboriginal self-determination. It lauded the various initiatives that had been created, but strongly emphasized the need for increased support for Aboriginal-controlled higher education institutions, including an "International Indigenous University."[15] On the contentious issue of the Aboriginal right to higher education, the RCAP observed:

One funding issue that arouses passionate and bitter debate is treaty rights to education. The numbered treaties promised education. Treaty nations and the federal government have been locked in a battle grounded in two widely divergent views of history. For treaty nations, education is a right that was negotiated in exchange for large tracts of traditional territory. In their view, this includes all levels of schooling, and that understanding is strongly embedded in the oral history that has come down from Aboriginal elders who were present at treaty negotiations and signings.

The federal government has denied that post-secondary education is a treaty right. It has applied the *Indian Act* provisions and its post-secondary funding policy to treaty nations on the same basis as First Nations that did not sign the Numbered Treaties. Students who do not live on a reserve often do not receive post-secondary education funding. Treaty nations argue that every treaty member should be entitled to the benefits, regardless of residence—in other words, that right to education is guaranteed and portable.

Over the past two decades, the Supreme Court of Canada has ruled in various cases that broad, just and liberal interpretation of treaties is in order, with due regard for the historical context in which they were signed. The historical context for Aboriginal peoples was one in which the buffalo and other animals that had sustained a migratory land-based economy were disappearing. Oral history tells us that Aboriginal leaders negotiating treaties were seeking education that would provide a livelihood sufficient to put them on an equal footing with the settlers in the new economy. Treaty nations argue that they were guaranteed an outcome from education that is not being honoured. Pauline Pelly, a Saskatchewan elder, voiced this view at the Federation of Saskatchewan Indian Nations treaty rights education symposium in October 1991: "Education was given to us. They promised that you will be very smart, like the cunning of the whiteman. The highest education that you can get, that is what they promised to us. That is what we wanted."

First Nations maintain that the spirit and intent of the treaties are as significant as the actual wording. The promise of a "schoolhouse on every reserve" represented what was the state-of-the-art education when the treaties were signed. And elders maintain that it was state-of-the-art

education that Aboriginal peoples negotiated. Supreme Court interpretations have lent support to Aboriginal contentions that the representations of
government at the time are as important as the actual words written down.

> *Recommendation 3.5.20: The Commission recommends that the
> government of Canada recognize and fulfill its obligation to treaty
> nations by supporting a full range of education services, including
> post-secondary education, for members of treaty nations where a
> promise of education appears in treaty texts, related documents or oral
> histories of the parties involved.*[16]

The Royal Commission noted the existence of four types of Aboriginal-
controlled institutions, one being a college, of which the Saskatchewan
Indian Federated College was recognized as "the largest and best known."[17]
A second type of institution was smaller, generally affiliated with a local
tribal council and focussed on brokering programs: institutions such as
Nicola Valley Institute of Technology, in British Columbia: Blue Quills,
Maskwachees, and Old Sun Colleges in Alberta; and Yellowquills College in
Manitoba. The third type was community learning centres that provided
upgrading and some distance-education courses. Finally, the fourth model
was a usually unaccredited institute that offered training in areas such as
First Nations self-government.[18]

While over a dozen mainstream universities offer programs in Native
Studies, RCAP noted that Aboriginal peoples did not enjoy the autonomy to
design programs that could best serve their needs. As well, the success rate
for Aboriginal students was far lower at mainstream universities than at
Aboriginal-controlled institutions. A number of elements make Aboriginal-
controlled higher education unique and contribute to the success of
Aboriginal students, such as culturally relevant approaches to education
that include an holistic balance of spiritual, physical, emotional, and
intellectual components. Contact with elders and meaningful integration
with community are other elements that ensure that First Nations higher
education is relevant and rewarding.[19] The RCAP urged universities to "continue their efforts to create a more hospitable environment for Aboriginal
students," and stated that part of the reason for the approximately 75%

success rate at Aboriginal-controlled institutions was that they had strong student support mechanisms, ties with the local communities, and access to elders and Aboriginal staff.[20]

One idea explored was to create an Aboriginal Peoples' International University, which could build upon a network of the existing Aboriginal-controlled institutions. Its goals could include articulating a unified vision of traditional knowledge, developing interpretations based on Indigenous concepts, and conducting applied research pertaining to Aboriginal self-government. It could be "a university without walls" that would rely heavily on modern communications technology such as the Internet.[21] Finally, the Royal Commission indicated that chronic underfunding and difficulties in receiving recognition within mainstream higher education were the biggest obstacles faced by Aboriginal-controlled institutions.

As Aboriginal peoples become a much greater proportion of the population of Canada, it is increasingly important to address Aboriginal higher education needs in order that First Nations can contribute properly to society. Dr. Ray Barnhardt, of the University of Alaska, described four models of Aboriginal higher education, based upon their ability to address the complex challenges. The most prevalent model is the "assimilationist model," in which programs for Indigenous people are controlled by the university system, and are designed with the premise that the goal of education is to assimilate Indigenous people into society. Such a regime, which places power and control in the hands of the mainstream, perpetuates dependence. This type of approach was envisaged in the 1993 Johnson Report on Saskatchewan Universities, in which First Nations higher education institutions were portrayed as merely feeder programs designed to bring First Nations students up to university standards.[22]

In a second "integrated model," universities provide a level of autonomy for the Indigenous program within the larger institution by means of advisory bodies and greater administrative independence. Success is possible where there is mutual respect and recognition, an example put forward being the First Nations House of Learning at the University of British Columbia.

A third "independent model" sees the establishment of tribal or regional colleges. While such institutions have the advantage of strong local control, because of their small size, they lack the critical mass of resources and have difficulty in mounting unique programs that will be recognized for accreditation. One possible way of surmounting this obstacle would be to establish strong networks that increase the faculty, student, and library resources available.

Finally, Barnhardt describes the "federated model" exemplified by the Saskatchewan Indian Federated College. Such an institution is financially and administratively separate from the university, yet benefits from having access to the resources and expertise of a mainstream university. Within such a milieu, the SIFC has been able to design a series of unique academic, cultural, and counselling programs that meet the needs of Indigenous students. At the same time, there are shortcomings, including the necessity of vetting its programs through the university for academic validation, and the perpetuation of the stereotype that achievement of quality is only possible through association with a non-Aboriginal university.[23]

Examining several independent, Aboriginal-controlled higher education institutions such as Gabriel Dumont Institute, Navajo Community College in the United States, Ilisimatusasfik University in Greenland, or Te Wananga o Raukawa in New Zealand, Barnhardt states that the commitment to community is the foremost objective of such institutions.

> It is the emphasis on empowerment that has been the most critical in moving the tribal colleges to seek status as independently accredited institutions of higher education.... Te Wananga o Raukawa, like most other Indigenous higher education initiatives, is of, by and for the community it serves. The Raukawa Trustees have made a deliberate effort to create an institution that is defined by, and has as its first consideration, the educational needs of the people they represent, and only secondarily have they concerned themselves with their relationship to other tertiary institutions.[24]

He notes that this commitment to community also manifests in the learning and management relationships between the institution of higher education and the community, in that

> the relationship between academic studies and the real world is treated as an interactive process, each contributing to the other in a cumulative fashion. Knowledge, rather than being fragmented into academic disciplines, is usually viewed in a *holistic framework* [emphasis added] and is acquired through a mutually constructive process drawing as much from experience as from books. The institutional structure generally reflects minimum hierarchy, and the boundaries between the various elements are often fluid, with students, faculty, administrators and community members moving back and forth across multiple roles.[25]

The close involvement of Aboriginal elders in these institutions is another sign of the close relationships with the community, but is also an area in which practice diverges sharply from the mainstream university. Overall, by supporting an holistic approach to education and being cognizant of the multiple needs of the students, these institutions are best able to address the needs of Indigenous peoples in their own communities. While Barnhardt acknowledges the need to meet generally accepted university standards, that should not be at the expense of the uniqueness of these institutions. At some point, there must be the proper balance of "think globally, act locally."[26]

In 1988, Indian Affairs initiated the Indian Studies Support Program (ISSP), designed to fund "Indian education organizations, Indian post-secondary institutions and other post-secondary institutions for the development and delivery of special programs for treaty/Status Indian students" as well as "the Saskatchewan Indian Federated College, as operational funding, to maintain a university-level focus on research and development in Indian Education and to deliver special programs."[27] The policy echoed to a major recommendation of the *Tradition and Education* report, which called for the creation of post-secondary institutions under the control of First Nations.

The intent of the ISSP was to improve Indian post-secondary education by providing funding to develop university-level programs aimed at enhancing Indian language and culture, and to "emphasize disciplines relevant to Indian self-government and appropriate labour markets, as determined in collaboration with Indian leaders and Indian educators."[28] Funding for ISSP would not exceed "12% of the department's total national annual post-secondary education allocation" and would include an initial operating budget for the Saskatchewan Indian Federated College of $4.7 million. As the only First Nations-controlled institution to evolve into a university institution fully recognized by the Association of Universities and Colleges of Canada (AUCC), SIFC will be examined in more detail. Several First Nations community-based tribal colleges, including Blue Quills, Maskwachees, Old Sun, and Red Crow, as well as various types of post-secondary programs, receive funding through ISSP (see Appendix B).

The Saskatchewan Indian Federated College was given legislative legitimacy in 1994 by the Federation of Saskatchewan Indian Nations' "Saskatchewan Indian Federated College Act" to "establish under First Nations government an autonomous degree-granting University College to serve First Nations people for the purpose of providing university-level education."[29] In 1993, the college was accepted as a full member of the Association of University and Colleges of Canada, the national recognition organization. From the 1980s until the early 1990s, the college was also affiliated with the American Indian Higher Education Consortium (AIHEC), the group representing Indian-controlled colleges in the United States. This provided an opportunity for SIFC to explore common goals and interests with similar institutions, particularly among northern plains tribes.

The AUCC's 1991 Commission of Inquiry on University Education found that Native peoples had benefited least from universities. Only 1.3% had earned a degree, versus 9.6% of the general population. While the AUCC acknowledged that many positive initiatives were being taken at university campuses, it stated that the "federal government deserves a great deal of credit for the special experiment of the Saskatchewan Indian Federated

College" and that the results indicated the need for continued support. (This credit was overstated, considering Indian Affairs' initial lack of support.) The AUCC expressed concern about jurisdictional wrangling between the federal and provincial governments, because "the college is in jeopardy and the students may suffer." The AUCC's report recommended that both governments employ an arbitrator to resolve their differences.[30]

By 1993-94, 54% of the PSSSP students attending university in Saskatchewan had enrolled at the SIFC. The college pursued a mandate of developing unique programs of benefit for Indians, such as the Indian Languages, Literature and Linguistics, and the Indian Fine Arts degree programs, both unique in North America; the Indian Social Work program accredited by the Canadian Association of Schools of Social Work; the Environmental Health Program developed in cooperation with the University of Regina's Faculty of Engineering; the First Nations Master of Business Administration and National School of Dentistry diploma, both under Memorandums of Agreement with the University of Saskatchewan; and the First Nations Banking program. At the graduate level, there are master's degree programs in Indian Studies, linguistics, and in social work. The college is a pioneer in community-based university education, assisting First Nations to design programs, such as Indian Career Community Counseling, Local Health Coordinators, Language Instructor's Certificate, and First Nations Development Studies, to best meet their needs.[31]

The SIFC has had to struggle with funding issues. Since Indian Affairs funding changed from a per capita to a fixed annual operating grant of $4.6 million in 1985-86, the college has seen its per-student funding decline to less than that of the University of Regina, although the grant increased to $5.6 million in 1995-96.[32] While provincial funding covering instruction for non-Aboriginal students attending SIFC grew from $100,000 to $600,000, the college estimated that the actual tuition and costs for educating non-treaty/ Status students in 1995-96 was in the range of $3 million.[33] Within the University of Regina system, where SIFC was one of three federated colleges, disparities were also noted. The SIFC's enrolment tripled from 1986 to 1995 and the number of student credit hours taught rose to 32,000, far more than the other federated colleges.[34] Campion and Luther colleges only taught about one-third of the class credit hours taken by their students, compared to about 90% at SIFC. However, despite the fact that SIFC taught more classes than Campion and Luther, its provincial grant amounted to only a quarter of theirs.[35]

Dr. Eber Hampton, president of the SIFC, maintained, "Most, but not all, university education in Canada today is education for assimilation" and that "we [First Nations] are prisoners of peace to the extent that we have allowed Eurocentric universities to monopolize higher education for our people."[36] Under the treaties, the Crown committed itself to the provision of education, which should be construed as including higher education, in order that First Nations could thrive and prosper. Hampton notes the university system not only "exerts a powerful influence on public thinking," but it also plays an important role in terms of providing research that becomes the basis for public policy.[37] He also observes that the cost of welfare "is more than twenty times as expensive as university education" when all the costs and benefits are totalled.

According to Dr. Eber Hampton, the time is now ripe for a further step in Indigenous higher education, putting in place a fully independent Indigenous university that would enter into relationships of equality with mainstream universities. Through its autonomy, yet rooted in the Aboriginal community, its programs would provide "a holistic view of education aimed at the development of the spiritual, emotional, physical and intellectual aspects of its students." He observed that the Canadian Council for Aboriginal Business, in its report to the Royal Commission on Aboriginal Peoples, saw the benefits of such an institution for the private sector and for Canada as a whole.[38]

Hampton notes the record of Aboriginal institutions in retaining and graduating Indian students. For example, the number of Aboriginal students completing degrees at the University of Regina has increased a hundredfold since the establishment of the Saskatchewan Indian Federated College. In pointing the way to the future, he advocates building upon existing strengths, including the "chartering of an Aboriginal university or universities" that could perform "the full range of university functions: teaching, research, community service and certification," all consistent with Aboriginal values and aspirations.[39]

———•◆•———

Approximately eighty other First Nations higher education programs of various types have also been funded through the Indian Studies Support Program. These programs generally received funding of between $10,000 and $700,000. Approximately 90% of these programs are located within First Nations communities. The primary success of these programs is that they have greatly increased access for First Nations students through on-reserve programs brokered from mainstream universities. In 2000, First Nations higher education institutions banded together under the Assembly of First Nations to form the National Association of Indigenous Institutes of Higher Learning (NAIIHL). The NAIIHL promotes self-determination over higher education, fosters cultural preservation, and addresses issues such as adequate funding and inter-institutional cooperation.[40]

With respect to Aboriginal post-secondary institutions generally, the 1997 Senate committee report commented: "The refusal to accredit and fund a range of First Nations institutions has meant that post-secondary education has become a growth industry for mainstream colleges and communities in which they are located." It noted that many Aboriginal educators felt they had a right and an obligation to "educate young Aboriginal people according to radically different standards based on their traditions and cultures."[41] The Senate report observed:

> The Saskatchewan Indian Federated College stands out among First Nations post-secondary institutions because of its tradition of academic excellence and the number of its Aboriginal academic personnel.... We believe that over the past twenty years, the Saskatchewan Indian Federated College has evolved into a post-secondary institution of significance, not only to the First Nations which founded and continue to nurture it, but also to Canada as a whole."[42]

The committee recommended that the federal government provide sufficient funding for First Nations institutions to meet their goals.

Aboriginal higher education associations, such as the First Nations Adult and Higher Education Consortium, which represents eight institutions such as Red Crow College in Alberta, have formed recently.[43] In 2000, the Assembly of First Nations conducted a national post-secondary education review. Part of this initiative included the "formation of an association of First Nations Higher and Adult Education Institutes" to look at issues such as accreditation.[44] Later that year, eighty representatives of higher education institutions and organizations formed the National Association of Indigenous Institutes of Higher Learning to "advance, advocate for and support post-secondary, technical, adult and related Indigenous education for the betterment of our institutions, communities and people."[45] The association also lobbies the federal government for capacity building funding, as well as exploring ways to protect intellectual rights to Aboriginal knowledge.[46]

———— ·•·•·•· ————

One of the major recommendations of the *Tradition and Education* report was turning control over education funding to First Nations. This resulted in shifting administration to bands, a movement that gained momentum under Minister Cadieux. In 1988, 73% of the 15,000 PSSSP students nationally had their programs administered by Indian organizations, with the remaining 27% administered by Indian Affairs. Of all the regions, Saskatchewan had the lowest participation, with only six of sixty-eight First Nations administering their own programs.[47] In Saskatchewan, funding was provided to enable First Nations to study the problems associated with the assumption of responsibility over education funding.

A Post-Secondary Education Study by the Touchwood/File Hills/ Qu'Appelle Tribal Council revealed some of the challenges in transferring administration of post-secondary programs to Indian organizations. The tribal council, which represented fifteen First Nations in southern Saskatchewan, polled 472 students funded through PSSSP at a cost of $3.2 million in 1988–89, about one-fifth of the total funding of $16 million for 1879 students in the province.[48] The study found that only 49% of students favoured administration by Indian organizations or bands, as opposed to Indian Affairs or other agencies such as the Saskatchewan Indian Federated

College. These individuals feared that a lack of strict guidelines and account-ability might lead to favouritism or unfair treatment at the band level.

The study concluded by recommending a combination of tribal council and band involvement. The tribal council would coordinate counselling training and the development of consistent policies. The band would be involved in determining priorities and in selecting the students who best filled those needs. Criteria would be established to outline the basis upon which students would be funded; for example, would students who succeeded be given higher priority over those who failed, and what levels of performance and eligibility would be required? Bands would have the option of proceeding on their own, apart from the tribal council, if they so desired.[49]

In March 1991, the Office of the Treaty Commissioner of Saskatchewan analyzed information it had requested from Indian Affairs pertaining to cost-benefit assessment. The assessment, which examined a four-year period, noted that Saskatchewan PSSSP enrolments had levelled off over a three-year period, with 1836 in 1987–88, 1872 in 1988–89 and 1897 in 1989–90. The exception to that trend was the Prince Albert area, where there was an increase in enrolments of 30%.[50] The treaty commissioner's 1992 report, entitled *Education as an Investment for Treaty Indians in Saskatche-wan: The Economic Costs and Benefits,* argued for much greater increases, rather than cutbacks in Indian higher education funding. It noted that between 1991 and 2011, the Indian population was expected to grow by 65.5% compared to 12.5% for the overall population. As well, in 1991, 50.6% of the Indian population was under twenty years of age, compared to 31.2% for the general population. A later study commissioned by the Federation of Saskatchewan Indian Nations, *Saskatchewan and Aboriginal Peoples in the 21st Century,* projected that by the year 2045, the Aboriginal population would reach 434,000, or 33% of the province's population.[51]

The report flagged a critical demographic issue. Given the long-term general trend of an aging Saskatchewan population, in which there will be more people over the age of sixty-five than under twenty by 2020, the need to develop a pool of qualified Aboriginal youth becomes even more pressing. The study referred to Aboriginal youth as "holding tremendous economic potential. This is a natural resource that could grow in importance as modern high-tech economies develop further." Elaborating on the economic and educational profile of Saskatchewan Indians, the study noted that only 24% had attained high school standing, compared to two thirds of the general population. However, in higher education, only 1% of Indians had graduated from university, compared to 8% in the general population. The demand to go on to university among Indian high school graduates was actually higher at 89%, compared to 78% in the general population.

Saskatchewan Treaty Commissioner Judge David Arnot observed that First Nations social conditions continued to indicate serious disparities. The unemployment rate among Saskatchewan Indians was 41%, compared to less than 10% for the province. In addition, 55% of Indian families fell below the poverty line, compared to 15% among the general public. Up to 40% of Indian adults experienced alcohol problems and the Saskatchewan Indian suicide rate was three times that of the non-Aboriginal population.[52]

The study examined a range of scenarios of education investment, including funding to improve school attendance, facilities, and participation at university, that would bring Indians to parity. It assumed that such investments would result in 99.1 million person years of employment, generate $1.94 billion in additional earnings, and reduce government transfers such as welfare by $238 million. In terms of education investment alone, the Treaty Commissioner concluded that the benefits outweighed costs by at least two to one.[53]

The Treaty Commissioner's report noted that 54.6% of the full-time Indian students were over the age of twenty-five. This contrasted with the general university population, in which 80% of the students were under twenty-five, with the majority coming to university out of high school and completing their first degrees prior to the age of twenty-five. Among the explanations for this phenomenon was that a high proportion of mature Indian students were attending university to take advantage of educational opportunities they had missed earlier. This was particularly true of recently reinstated Bill C-31 First Nations students, 64% of whom were over the age of twenty-five and who had only recently gained access to PSSSP funding. As a subgroup, the participation rate of single parents with dependents had increased by 42% over the study period. However, they were also among the most costly in terms of funding, with requirements to house, feed and care for the dependents adding 60% to costs.[54] Although financing single-parent students with dependents cost up to $5000 more, such costs would be recovered within one to thirteen years of the family's being taken off welfare rolls.[55] The assessment determined that the pent-up demand by older students, as well as an increase of single parents with dependents, were the main reasons why overall costs appeared to be spiralling without concomitant educational results. The assessment also observed that Indian higher education participation at 69 per 1000 was still only about half that of the general population at 141 per 1000. As well, Indian students were only one-sixth as likely to attend on a part-time basis.

Finally, the study determined that abuse of the program by the "professional student syndrome" was insignificant at 1%[56] and that there was "an increasing student preference for Aboriginal-controlled institutions" such as the Saskatchewan Indian Federated College.[57] Nationally, PSSSP enrolments in 1990–91 stood at 21,300, an increase of 13% over the previous year, and in 1991–92, 22,500 students enrolled, a further 5% increase. In 1991, Indian Affairs announced the addition of $320 million over five years to the national post-secondary education budget.[58] By 1997–98, PSSSP enrolments were up to 27,000 with a program budget of $276 million, with almost 100% of funding now being administered by First Nations.

———•◆•———

First Nations Indian political leaders assert that education at all levels is a right gained through treaty, and that treaty Indians have an exclusive trust relationship with the federal government under which those services must be provided.[59] The federal government has consistently maintained that post-secondary education funding is a social benefit only. First Nations also claim that provinces have no right or jurisdiction to become involved with, or otherwise interfere with, Indian education delivery.

The legal argument for the treaty right to higher education rests on the rules of treaty interpretation, the fiduciary obligation of the Crown, and the unique constitutional position of First Nations.[60] Lower court cases to date have leaned towards interpreting First Nations higher education as a treaty right and a federal responsibility. The plaintiff in the *Greyeyes* case, Deanna Greyeyes of the Muskeg Lake Reserve in Saskatchewan, received post-secondary funding from Indian Affairs to attend the University of Calgary in 1974. When the Department of National Revenue categorized such funding as taxable income, Greyeyes appealed. Judge Mahoney ruled that the scholarship was provided by Indian Affairs under a treaty to the band and should therefore be considered to be non-taxable property of an Indian.[61]

A legal opinion prepared by the Assembly of First Nations pointed out that in the Supreme Court case *Mitchell v. Peguis Indian Band* (1990), the court referred to higher education as "part of the consideration for the cession of Indian Lands." The opinion called for the courts to provide a "broad and liberal interpretation" of the treaties as the Supreme Court had determined in the *R. v. Sparrow* (1990) case.[62] In *R v. Agawa* case (1988), the Ontario Court of Appeal ruled that the treaties were intended to treat the Indians fairly and should be interpreted liberally, as the Honour of the Crown was in question. In *Nowegijick v. R.* (1983), the court decided that Aboriginal understandings of treaty provisions are to be given strong weight in treaty interpretation, and ambiguities should be resolved in favour of the Indians.[63]

Guerin v. R. (1984) established that the nature of the federal government's fiduciary relation towards Indians must be one of goodwill and must take into consideration the solemn obligations undertaken when the land was transferred by the Indians to the Crown. *R. v. Sparrow* (1990) indicated that treaty relationships were meant to be progressive and evolve over time to suit the changing times. Finally, if post-secondary education is accepted as a treaty right, then it would be protected by section 35 of the *Constitution Act,* 1982.[64]

The thinking about importance and rights involving First Nations higher education has greatly evolved over recent years. The Assembly of First Nations' 1988 report, *Tradition and Education,* asserted jurisdiction and sovereignty over post-secondary education, and, in doing so, introduced a major turning point in the discourse.[65] The AFN noted the vital link between higher education and self-government and called for exclusive Aboriginal control to be exerted. The report praised the Saskatchewan Indian Federated College as "a practical example of the implementation of First Nations self-government and self-determination."[66] With the federal government failing to enact appropriate legislation, the *Tradition and Education* report pointed out that "A test case seeking a declaration that Constitutionally the federal government has an obligation to resource education for First Nations citizens" could be pursued. It cautioned, however, that "an adverse ruling is difficult if not possible to negotiate away."[67] The fear of the Supreme Court's arriving at a negative or narrow interpretation, and the implications of that on the gains made so far, gave pause for thought about rushing into legal action.

Chapter 6

A New Deal

IRST NATIONS DISSATISFACTION with universities' ability to meet their higher education needs continues. A recent example is outlined by professors Dennis McPherson and Douglas Rabb in the article "Restoring the Interpretive Circle: Community-based Research and Education," where the authors refer to the situation that arose at Lakehead University in connection with a grant for USD $250,000 from the Rockefeller Foundation to develop Native philosophy. With the help of this funding, a First Nations-based Ayaangwaamizin Academy of Indigenous Learning was established to stimulate philosophical inquiry. In 1999, sixteen Aboriginal students involved in this process applied to the qualifying year of Lakehead's Native and Canadian Philosophy MA program. All sixteen applicants were rejected, and the following year, Lakehead closed what was expected to be Canada's first graduate program in Aboriginal philosophy.[1] To McPherson and Rabb, the message from the university was clear: "It has told Indians they do not belong there."[2]

They were not the first academics to express disappointment. In reflecting on his twenty-five year career, Howard Adams viewed much of university teaching as an exercise in neo-colonialism: "there are Native Studies programs at almost every large university in Canada and many teacher institutes offering special programs to train Natives to be teachers. But their perspectives and ideologies are quite consistent with mainstream courses.... All of these courses indoctrinate Native students to conservative middle class ideologies. They are intended towards creating an Aboriginal bourgeoisie."[3] McPherson and Rabb observe: "Adams represents a growing number of Aboriginal academics who have spent their careers encouraging Native students to pursue post-secondary education, only to find that the system has let them down."[4] Marie Battiste and James (Sa'ke'j) Henderson from the University of Saskatchewan also express reservations: "At best Canadian universities and educational systems teach this double consciousness to Indigenous students. Canadian educational systems view Indigenous heritage, identity and thought as inferior to Eurocentric heritage, identity and thought.... Educators still know very little about how Indigenous students are raised and socialized in their homes and communities, and even less about how Indigenous heritage is traditionally transmitted."[5]

While over a dozen mainstream universities offer programs in Native Studies, the report of the Royal Commission on Aboriginal Peoples acknowledged that Aboriginal peoples still did not enjoy the autonomy to design programs that could best serve their needs. As well, the success rate for Indigenous students was far lower than at Aboriginal-controlled institutions. It urged universities to "continue their efforts to create a more hospitable environment for Aboriginal students."[6] The RCAP recognized that while universities are attempting to integrate Aboriginal needs by creating programs such as Native Studies, student completion rates are unacceptably low, often because Aboriginal students feel "isolated in a hostile environment where professors and students express racist attitudes and opinions."[7]

The 2002 report *Best Practices in Increasing Aboriginal Post-Secondary Enrolment Rates,* prepared for the Council of Ministers of Education,[8] acknowledged that "Almost all Aboriginal education dollars are spent in universities and programs that are not under Aboriginal control. Many of the interviews conducted and much of the literature reviewed for this study demonstrate that whenever Aboriginals are given control over their own programs or institutions, there have been higher rates of success in Aboriginal enrolment and graduation."[9] It concludes, "Best Practices for Aboriginal post-secondary enrolment and retention strategies depend upon Aboriginals exerting control over their own education. A fundamental shift in the postsecondary system would depend on the initiation of increased Aboriginal control at the institutional level."[10] *Best Practices* noted concern about "often poor or hostile public perception of programs and initiatives geared toward Aboriginal people." This indicates the need for a campaign of public education and raising of awareness.

———•◆•———

Approximately eighty First Nations higher education programs of various types are funded on a project-driven basis through the Indian Studies Support Program, receiving between $10,000 and $700,000 per project. About 90% of these programs are located within First Nations communities. The primary success of these programs is that they have greatly increased access for First Nations students to on-reserve programs generally brokered from mainstream universities.

In eastern Canada, where a tradition of post-Confederation treaty making did not exist, First Nations control over post-secondary education is the least developed. In the Maritimes, there are no independent, Aboriginal-controlled, higher education institutes. The Micmac-Malecite Institute, opened in 1981, is the only centre for Aboriginal higher education in the Maritimes. Affiliated with the University of New Brunswick, the institute offers a BEd degree to train Aboriginal teachers, a First Nations Business Administration Certificate, and a preparatory Bridging Year. As well, in Quebec, no major Indigenous-controlled post-secondary institutions have developed since the closing of Manitou Community College in 1979. While the James Bay Cree control their own elementary and secondary education system, they partner with Heritage College for delivery of adult distance-education courses.

In Ontario, the Aboriginal Institutes Consortium, representing nine institutions, was formed to collaborate on common issues such as achieving recognition and accreditation, and obtaining core funding. The institutes delivered 150 programs to 17,906 students over the past seven years. One member of the consortium, the First Nations Technical Institute, was established in 1985 and has offered programs including public administration, social services worker training, community work, health work, small business, computer software, and aviation.

In Manitoba, much of the emphasis has been on establishing "access programs" to increase Aboriginal participation in the province's mainstream public universities. The University of Manitoba has made a major investment in providing improved access. Its Aboriginal Access Program has two recruiters, and coordinates a variety of student support initiatives including tutoring, counselling, and mentoring. Access to professional programs at the University of Manitoba includes the Aboriginal Business Education Program, Engineering Access Program, Social Work Distance Education, Health Careers Access Program, and Faculty of Education Access Program.[11] The university, which has as many as 2400 Aboriginal students, officially intends to position itself as the pre-eminent institution for attracting Aboriginal students for higher education in Canada. The success of the access strategy has shown itself not only in enrolments, but also in improved Aboriginal student retention, a rate now in excess of 60%.

Yellowquill College, operated by the Dakota Ojibway Council and located in Winnipeg, is the only First Nations-controlled post-secondary institution in Manitoba. The college, which offers a range of preparatory and technical courses, is founded upon the principle that First Nations have the right to determine and offer what they deem to be appropriate programs. In 1993, the Assembly of Manitoba Chiefs passed a resolution calling for a First Nations-controlled post-secondary institute to be established in Manitoba. The City of Winnipeg has expressed openness to creating an urban Indian reserve that could be used for such a purpose. However, the idea remains controversial.[12] The chiefs are also now considering how Manitoba's recently created University College of the North can serve their needs.

In Saskatchewan, First Nations University of Canada (originally Saskatchewan Indian Federated College) was born at the initiative of Saskatchewan First Nations elders and leaders who wished to see the formation of an institution of higher learning that would mirror their philosophies, languages, history, and concepts of government. That institution would assist First Nations to find their place in the modern world while keeping First Nations heritage intact. The SIFC was considered a bold experiment in Aboriginal-controlled post-secondary education. While it has enjoyed successes, core funding arrangements have proven inadequate to meet the growing demands of First Nations in the province, let alone the entire country.[13]

In Alberta, tribal colleges, including Red Crow Community College, Old Sun Community College, Blue Quills First Nations College, Maskwachees Cultural College, Bullhead Adult Education Centre, Nechi Training, Research and Health Promotion Institute, Nakoda Education, Pikani Post-Secondary Education, and Yellowhead Tribal Council Education, were formed to provide culturally appropriate education on the reserves. For example, Red Crow College, established in 1986, emphasizes Blackfoot culture, traditions, and knowledge. It also offers programs in leadership training and traditional land use, as well as teacher training in cooperation with the University of Lethbridge and social work in partnership with the University of Calgary.

In British Columbia, the Union of British Columbia Indian Chiefs (UBCIC) voted in 1991 to set up the Institute of Indigenous Government (IIG), an Indigenous-controlled post-secondary institute dedicated to developing self-government skills. In 1993, the province agreed to accredit IIG as a provincial institute under the *College and Institute Act*, and the IIG's Board of Governors was appointed by the province, acting upon nominations from the UBCIC. The Nicola Valley Institute of Technology (NVIT), established in 1983 by the First Nations of the Nicola Valley area, in 1995 also became a provincial institute similar to the IIG. Today, NVIT also operates as a private institution under the *British Columbia College and Institute Act,* with 230 students, 80% of whom are Aboriginal, housed in a new $9-million facility made possible by provincial funding.

Issues of jurisdiction have arisen across the country. In Quebec and the Maritimes, where few First Nations-controlled institutions exist, mainstream universities, some of which receive ISSP funding, play the dominant role in post-secondary education delivery. Standing in stark contrast, section 6 of the *Mi'kmaq Education Act* (1998), concerning jurisdiction, states: "The participating First Nations shall have jurisdiction with respect to post-secondary student support funding for members residing on and off First Nations land." In Quebec, the First Nations Education Council, based at Wendake, notes that the AFN's document, "First Nations Educational Jurisdiction 2004," called for each region to "establish structures/bodies for the implementation of educational jurisdiction at the local and regional levels." Post-secondary education was identified as one of those areas.[14]

In 1998, the Anishinabek Nation in Ontario signed a *Framework for an Education Agreement in Principle* that does not limit or abrogate any Aboriginal or treaty rights, the first of its kind in the province. From the perspective of these First Nations, who represent about 2100 post-secondary students, the agreement is intended to restore their jurisdiction over education matters and enable them to enter into further self-government agreements in the future.[15] The agreement also sets out the relationships between the federal and Ontario government, although the latter has not actively participated in the negotiations.[16]

In Manitoba, the Assembly of Manitoba Chiefs signed the *Framework Agreement on Indian Education in Manitoba* with the federal government in 1990. In one of the introductory clauses of the agreement, federal refusal to accept responsibility for post-secondary education is acknowledged: "And whereas attempts by the parties to negotiate certain issues relating to treaty rights and to post-secondary education have not given rise to acceptable rights ... these issues may therefore be addressed outside the scope of this Framework Agreement." This leaves the province of Manitoba, which is not a party to the agreement, to play a principal role.

The Saskatchewan Indian Federated College, which covers the province through regional campuses and community-based offerings, was given legislative legitimacy in 1994 by the Federation of Saskatchewan Indian Nations' *Saskatchewan Indian Federated College Act,* establishing "under First Nations government an autonomous degree-granting University College to serve First Nations people for the purpose of providing university-level education."[17] The SIFC was accepted as a full member of the Association of University and Colleges of Canada in 1993 on the basis of meeting certain criteria, such as being able to operate free of political interference. Its renaming to First Nations University of Canada in 2003 is reflective of SIFC's original vision and its funding as a national institution.

In Alberta, the principal approach has been to establish regional tribal colleges, established and controlled by First Nations to meet local community needs. Nine tribal college and post-secondary institutes, along with Yellowquill College in Manitoba, have formed the First Nations Adult and Higher Education Consortium to "provide quality adult and higher education controlled entirely by people of the First Nations" as well as to set accreditation standards. Red Crow College is also a member of the American Indian Higher Education Consortium.[18]

In British Columbia's *Aboriginal Post-Secondary Education and Training Policy Framework,* the province's legal interpretation of its obligations towards Aboriginal post-secondary education is outlined:

> In the area of education, because the *Indian Act,* section 4(3) limits the application of the Act to Indians between the ages of 7 and 17 ordinarily resident on a reserve, the responsibility for post-secondary education and for Aboriginal people has resided with the province through legislation regarding public post-secondary education and training.[19]

The provincial legislation referred to is British Columbia's *Private Post-Secondary Education Act.* The policy framework was approved in 1995 after a series of forums with Aboriginal political organizations, including the Association of Aboriginal Post-secondary Institutions (AAPSI), which represents fifteen institutions enrolling 1500 students. Noting that the federal government does not assume responsibility, British Columbia has moved aggressively into the perceived void of First Nations higher education jurisdiction. At the same time, an agreement has been negotiated with the federal government to provide 25% of the funding required to bring First Nations post-secondary education to parity. This approach has been successful because the province has been able to offer major operational funding as well as accreditation, something not possible under the Indian Studies Support Program. The First Nations have tacitly permitted such funding arrangements, perceiving they better meet the immediate needs of their culturally diverse and geographically dispersed communities. In the North, institutions such as Arctic College have been created that can serve a far-flung population and keep students closer to their home communities.

Generally, First Nations in all regions of Canada are issuing declarations and enacting legislation that protects their jurisdiction over all areas of education. However, the federal government's refusal to accept a fiduciary responsibility for First Nations post-secondary education implies that Aboriginal institutions will continue to be forced to partner with mainstream universities and colleges for recognition and additional resources. The forced reorganization of the Institute of Indigenous Government, "BC's first autonomous degree-granting Indigenous-controlled post-secondary institution" by the Province of British Columbia, following a 1998 review, suggests that First Nations control in that case was ephemeral.[20] Should the First Nations eventually feel that such partnership arrangements no longer meet their needs, it is presumed that under First Nations' inherent sovereignty, their own institutions could be set up, although this would entail challenging organizational, financial, and jurisdictional issues.

The AFN's "First Nations Post-Secondary Education Review" found that of post-secondary students nationally, only approximately half were enrolled in university institutions. For example, in 1993, of a total of 17,699 post-secondary students, 9023 or 50.9% were enrolled in universities, and in 1997, of a total of 23,205 post-secondary students, the proportion of university students stood virtually unchanged at 11,793 or 50.8%.[21] That year, these students were predominately enroled in three main fields: general arts and sciences (25.8%), education (20%), and social sciences and services (16.7%). The areas of least representation were mathematics and physical sciences (1.1%) and agriculture and bio-sciences (1.4%).[22]

One can question whether post-secondary participation of First Nations students is comparable to that of non-Aboriginal students. A closer look suggests that the federal government has fallen far short of achieving its policy goal of parity of First Nations participation in post-secondary education. According to recent Department of Indian Affairs data, 26,800 First Nations students were funded through their Post-Secondary Student Support Program in 2000–01.[23]

According to this breakdown, approximately 13,400 First Nations students were enrolled in universities in 2000, including both full- and part-time students, of which the latter constitute approximately 10%.[24] In terms of the overall First Nations population, total numbers in 2000 would be approximately 683,200. The participation rate in higher education in 2000 was therefore 13,400 out of 683,200,[25] or approximately 2% of the First Nations population.

The overall Canadian population of Canada in July 2003 was approximately 31,625,000.[26] According to the Association of Universities and Colleges of Canada, which represents over eighty higher education institutions, the number of Canadians enrolled in universities in 2003–04 is 1,028,000.[27] The mainstream participation rate, after excluding 16,000 First Nations students, is 1,012,000 out of 31,625,000 or 3.2%. Comparing this to the First Nations participation rate of 2%, one concludes that the First Nations participation rate in higher education is only 60% that of mainstream society.

To arrive at complete statistics on post-secondary education, the other component of community colleges must be added. According to the Association of Canadian Community Colleges, which represents 147 institutions, they have an enrollment of 2,400,00 students.[28] Added to approximately 1,000,000 non-Aboriginal students in Canadian universities, the total number of Canadian students enrolled in post-secondary education is approximately 3,400,000. Of a total population of 31,625,000, this represents a post-secondary education participation rate of 10.8%. The total number of First Nations post-secondary students, including those at universities and community colleges in 2000, was 26,800. Out of a total First Nations population of 683,200, this would represent a participation rate of 3.9%. This means that the First Nations overall post-secondary participation rate of 3.9% is only 36%, or just over a third of the mainstream society's rate of 10.8%.

Given the lack of growth in the post-secondary budget, which has increased only at approximately 2% per year, consistent with overall Indian Affairs budget increases, this funding has not kept pace with increases in university tuitions, with the result that fewer First Nations students are able to be sponsored. The Assembly of First Nations noted that the number of funded students had fallen from a high of 27,157 in 1999 to 25,075 in 2003.[29] The implications of these figures are, first, that the federal government has fallen far short of its stated policy objective of achieving parity in post-secondary participation by First Nations, and, second, that the disparity is beginning to widen. In order to achieve such parity, the federal government would have to triple its current level of funding, bringing it from the $293 million in 2000–01 to nearly $900 million.

Another controversial issue has arisen recently over the decision by the Canada Revenue Agency in 2004 to tax First Nations post-secondary education payments. Interestingly, the impetus for this move came from the Department of Indian Affairs, whose spokesperson reiterated the federal government's long-standing opinion that such programs are "a matter of social policy, not of treaty rights."[30] Such a position overlooks the fact that the most recent legal decisions have supported the concept that such rights flow from Indian treaties and hence should not be taxed. Such a move reveals the fundamental contradiction of the department—can it be both trustee of First Nations rights and arm of the federal government? As of the time of writing, the Canada Revenue Agency has indefinitely postponed plans to implement the tax. However, the tax has not been declared invalid.

The other area of concern in a comprehensive post-secondary program, apart from the funding of students to pursue education, is the funding of Aboriginal-controlled post-secondary institutions themselves. According to the Association of Universities and Colleges of Canada, the total amount of funding of various sorts to Canadian universities, be it in tuitions, research funds, capital funds, or government transfers for 2003–04, amounts to $23,518,660,000.[31] The leading sources of this funding were transfers from other levels of government, provincial governments, and own-source revenue. Applying this amount to the approximately 1,000,000 non-Aboriginal students in universities suggests that these global resources translate to roughly $23,500 per student.

TABLE 5: Total Global Revenues Per Student at Sample Universities[32]

INSTITUTION	TOTAL (YEAR)	ENROLMENTS (YEAR)	REVENUES (PER STUDENT)
Univ. of Toronto	$1,143,395,000 (01–02)	47,265 (01–02)	$24,190
Univ. of Manitoba	463,459,000 (01–02)	23,618 (01–02)	19,623
Univ. of Saskatchewan	524,000,000 (00–01)	20,493 (00–01)	25,569
Univ. of Alberta	919,785,000 (01–02)	32,246 (01–02)	28,524
First Nations Univ.	16,337,381 (01–02)	1,200 (01–02)	13,614

The average per-student resources of the four sampled universities are $24,476. When compared to this average, the total revenue of the First Nations University, Canada's national university for First Nations, is only 64% of the level of resources received by those province-funded public universities. The First Nations University's revenue comes primarily from the Indian Studies Support Program, comprising 33.4% of its overall revenues, with student tuitions (21.8%) and "non-operational" funding (15.2%) constituting the other major sources. Despite the recent construction of its facility, made possible only through long-term leasing of half the facility to Indian Affairs, the institution still does not receive funding for capital development or maintenance. This analysis of funding raises other questions, such as whether Aboriginal peoples, who constitute 3.3% of

Canada's population, benefit fairly from the $23.5 billion in total revenues accorded to Canadian universities.[33] If Aboriginal peoples were receiving their 3.3% proportion, they would be benefiting from approximately $775 million in funding resources for higher education alone. Adding an additional proportion for the full range of post-secondary education that includes community colleges would at least double that amount.[34] Métis and Inuit populations, who do not have access to the same programs as First Nations, or capital funds for existing or new facilities, experience even greater disparity. These statistics bare the shabby treatment accorded to Aboriginal-controlled post-secondary education in terms of government policy. The underfunding of Aboriginal-controlled institutions, along with the expectation that mainstream universities can fill the need, is an unacceptable evasion of the real issue of failing to fully empower Aboriginal post-secondary education.

In examining post-secondary education funding needs, the Assembly of First Nations stated, "Using conservative estimates, a total of $880, 305, 332 is required" as follows:[35]

TABLE 6: First Nation Post-Secondary Funding Required

$614,199,530	for the Post-secondary Student Support Program
$73,703,944	for the Indian Studies Support Program
$110,555,915	for First Nation Post-Secondary Institutes
$79,845,939	for administration
$2,000,000	for the development of a database

Such figures expose the underfunding of Aboriginal-controlled institutions when compared to mainstream universities. Under such conditions, Aboriginal students will continue to underperform, and it will be extremely unlikely that they will exceed their current miniscule proportion among the ranks of PhDs or medical doctors and other professionals for many generations.

On March 21, 2000, Assembly of First Nations National Chief Phil Fontaine met with Finance Minister Paul Martin to discuss the federal budget and raised the issue of First Nations post-secondary student underfunding. The AFN reported that Martin "was unaware of this situation and agreed to support increased PSE funding if shown evidence. The National Chief agreed to provide a list of names."[36] A national telephone survey conducted as part of the First Nations Post-Secondary Education Review identified a list of 9465 individuals who fell within this category.[37] The review also stated: "It is estimated that 39,160 First Nations students will require post-secondary assistance in 2005–2006. For this reason, post-secondary education has become a high political priority for this organization [AFN]."[38]

The Post-Secondary Student Support Program has managed to achieve only one-third of its goal of attaining post-secondary participation rates comparable with mainstream society. The Assembly of First Nations points out that funding by PSSSP had not substantially increased since 1995–96, and living allowances have not kept pace with increases in the cost of living. If First Nations are to truly enjoy the full benefits of higher education, including access to effective Aboriginal-controlled institutions, existing post-secondary funding should be immediately tripled to at least $1 billion annually.

A former chief of the Assembly of First Nations, Matthew Coon-Come, had also noted that the Liberal government had not kept its promise to remove the cap on post-secondary funding, made in the 1993 Liberal "red book":

> A Liberal Government will remove the cap on postsecondary educa-
> tion specifically to provide adequate funding for Aboriginal students
> accepted at colleges, universities and vocational institutes, and in
> adult education programs and professional degree programs.[39]

The Assembly of First Nations has indicated that lifting the cap on First Nations post-secondary education will be a tangible way in which the new government can demonstrate its purported commitment to embracing Aboriginal issues.

The latest federal initiative of the Liberal government for discussing Aboriginal education policy change, the Round Table on Life Long Learning, aims "to seek transformative change." Participants on the Round Table were drawn from a wide spectrum of both Aboriginal and non-Aboriginal experts. The recommendations would become the rationale for increased funding in the Kelowna Accord, signed with Prime Minister Paul Martin and provincial and territorial leaders in November 2005. The Accord planned to provide $500 million over five years to enable First Nations post-secondary institutions to be funded at equitable levels and to address inflationary costs and enrolment increases.

The AFN *Background Paper on Lifelong Learning,* prepared for discussion with First Ministers in 2005, noted:

> It is time for governments to fund and support the development of First Nations institutions of higher learning that are controlled by First Nations peoples. A variety of First Nations controlled colleges, institutes and community learning centres have already been developed. However, these institutions experience a chronic lack of funding and also the reluctance of mainstream post-secondary institutions to recognize their courses and certificates/degrees. Courses and programs offered by these First Nations institutes of higher learning are highly relevant and valued by First Nations communities; it has been demonstrated that these institutions provide a supportive learning environment and students are encouraged to persist and complete their courses/programs.[40]

The 2004 auditor general's report called upon Indian and Northern Affairs to take action to eliminate the education gap between First Nations and mainstream society. It identified significant weaknesses in the Post-Secondary Student Support Program's management and accountability framework, including the lack of basic statistical data on programs offered and student enrolment and completion. The scrutiny levelled on First Nations education over past years and the demand for more accountability for results have placed a great deal of pressure on Indian and Northern Affairs to demonstrate that gains are being made for the funds expended. First Nations and Indian and Northern Affairs Canada must work together to find a mechanism through which data can be produced and accountability guaranteed.

The example of the tribal college system in the United States has lessons to offer. Six American Indian tribal colleges initially formed the American Indian Higher Education Consortium (AIHEC) in 1973. Tribal colleges were inspired by the self-determination movement of the 1960s and the realization that mainstream universities were not meeting the needs of American Indians living on reservations. The first, the Navajo (now Dine) College, was established in 1968. Today, AIHEC includes thirty-one tribally mandated and four intertribal universities and colleges that enrol over 33,000 students whose average age is twenty-seven and are 70% female.

In the United States, American Indian and Alaska Natives are eligible for special funding through the Bureau of Indian Affairs, which offered over $30 million in 1994 to 15,000 Native American students in the form of grants averaging $2412 per student.[41] Tribal colleges are provided government per-student funding under the *Tribally Controlled Community College Assistance Act* (1978) and later the *Tribally Controlled College and University Act,* a funding initiative sponsored by President Bill Clinton in 1996 and renewed by President George Bush in 2002. The *Act* recognizes federal responsibilities to assist post-secondary institutions on Indian lands, as they are not eligible for state grants. In 1983, the *Act* allotted $5280 per American Indian full-time student (approximately $8000 in 2002 funds). By 1998, the amount allocated was USD$6000, still substantially less than the average at mainstream community colleges.[42] The American Indian Higher Education Consortium also has its own Tribal College Fund, which seeks funding from corporate and philanthropic sources such as the Carnegie and Kellogg foundations to target specific priorities identified by the colleges. In addition, private sources such as Buffy Sainte-Marie's Nihewan Foundation have provided scholarships that have enabled some American Indian students to complete doctoral degrees.[43]

Tribal colleges are successful not only because they provide a culturally affirming environment, but also because they are responsive to local community dynamics. One of the successful impacts of tribal colleges has been to assist with the economic development of the reservations. This is accomplished in various ways, including employment, local expenditure, workforce skills development, and fostering entrepreneurship and small business development through Tribal Business Information Centres. Local land use and economic opportunities can be researched, and technology such as Internet usage can be introduced. The colleges, the majority of which offer two-year programs, employ an average of eighty-one faculty and staff and generate $2.1 million in salaries per college. Reservations in which tribal colleges exist show higher rates of employment and economic growth, and greater numbers of students remain in the community, making contributions that might otherwise have been directed towards urban centres. For example, the 63% employment rate of graduates of Stonechild College in Rocky Boy Reservation, Montana, stands in contrast to the reservation's overall 28% employment rate. Other positive impacts of post-secondary programs on reservation communities include reduction of dependence on welfare, less drug and alcohol use, and reduced rates of suicide.[44]

In spite of insufficient funding, over half the tribal colleges are venturing into using distance-education technology such as Internet-based instruction. Haskell University in Kansas has a distance-education program; Bay Mills Community College, Michigan, offers fifty online courses; and North Dakota tribal colleges have formed a "virtual learning community." This approach recognizes the reality that many students have family or job-related obligations, and that Internet-based instruction offers necessary flexibility. Through the Internet, a virtual library can be created and shared to provide a critical mass of materials for participating institutions. All the institutions have found that distance-education technology has enhanced the achievement of their tribal college mission.[45]

American Indian students who attend a tribal college before transferring to a four-year institution were four times as likely to complete their degrees as those who entered as first-year students at mainstream universities.[46] In this sense, tribal colleges have similar successes as historically black colleges, which have demonstrated significantly higher levels of program completion rates for American Blacks. Tribal colleges are "creating bright circles of hope on their reservations."[47] They have not only revolutionized Indian education, but have also become major engines of change in American Indian communities. Regional accreditation agencies in the United States have recognized the validity of judging tribal colleges based upon their abilities to meet their unique mission. This model of Indigenous higher education is spreading around the globe with a network, the World Indigenous Higher Education Consortium, founded at Kananaskis, Alberta, in 2002, representing initiatives in Australia, Canada, Mexico, New Zealand, Sweden, and the United States.

Finally, a cautionary lesson about the pitfalls of Aboriginal control and governance should be learned from the experience at the First Nations University of Canada (FNUC), where twenty-three of the board's thirty-one members were political appointees of the Federation of Saskatchewan Indian Nations. On February 17, 2005, board chairman Morley Watson suspended three senior administrative officers of the First Nations University, stating this was necessary in order to investigate allegations of corruption. The repercussions of this controversial political intervention included firing and resignations of faculty and staff who spoke against the actions, turmoil among students, and questions about the institution's credibility within the university community.

The original vision of SIFC had been a broad one: a high-quality university institution that sought the best knowledge of both Aboriginal and non-Aboriginal worlds and was to serve a national and international clientele. A highly capable, talented, and committed team of Aboriginal academics had been gradually drawn to the institution, and were on the verge of bringing the First Nations University to the lofty heights it had aspired to, creating programs equal to, if not better than, Aboriginal programs in mainstream universities. Credibility was such that funding agencies were contemplating major investments in expanded programming. However, the intrusion of February 2005 into the operations of the FNUC revealed its weaknesses.

The board, using unrestrained power, was able to set in motion a series of events that, due to a lack of checks and balances, caused the institution to collapse like a house of cards. It is clear that the board did not properly assess the situation or anticipate the consequences. A year and a half after the initial intrusion, there has been no reporting of major corruption, despite an audit estimated to have cost $500,000. In retrospect, the actions amounted to a political takeover and radical narrowing of the institution's mission. The international program was disbanded and plans to establish a doctoral program in Indigenous Studies were abandoned. These were replaced by an emphasis on delivering teaching programs to First Nations communities in the province. Partners in the academic enterprise, such as the University of Regina, stood by impotently. In a normal situation, one would have expected that checks and balances would come into play to prevent such a disastrous fallout.

At the risk of making the board judgement appear to be the major culprit, it must be pointed out that the foundation for the calamitous fall of FNUC was laid by the federal and provincial governments that underfunded the institution, making it impossible to achieve its ambitious mission. For example, the contribution of the Saskatchewan government to FNUC is to compensate for the enrolment of non-Aboriginal students, and in that sense is not directed towards First Nations education.

At a symposium on November 10, 2005, at which Aboriginal scholars from across Canada met to discuss the crisis at FNUC, participants were reminded about the colonialist nature of Canada's history, the usurpation of land and resources, and relegation of Aboriginal peoples to an underpriviledged class. One of the unique characteristics that distinguishes the FNUC from all other institutions is that it is a university of a colonized people. The events at FNUC, and the trauma produced as factions futilely lash out against one another, is typical of lateral violence that occurs within colonized populations. Others observed a trend towards fundamentalism in all levels of Aboriginal education—a growing rejection of, and intolerance towards, non-Aboriginal views.

One of the high points of the symposium was a healing testimonial by Ojibway elder Bev Shawanda, who recounted her experiences of being abused and her personal struggle to overcome its impacts. She pointed out that in order to overcome the trauma involved, it is first necessary to recognize that the abuse is occurring before being in a position to rise above it. She pointed out that institutions such as FNUC should be safe places where students can learn about, become empowered over, and resolve to rise above not only the personal, but also collective, trauma of colonialism.

Concerns that the governance of FNUC had been tied too closely to the FSIN had been long-standing. Doug Cuthand, the first board chairman of SIFC, noted that the intent of the original board was to have Aboriginal chiefs replace administrators once the institution's direction had been set. But the board chair, without the benefit of any studies, defended the political board, stating: "We have our own traditions and ways of doing things and sometimes that is not always kosher with organizations," but that the changes would result in "a top notch university."[48] However, in the eyes of the Association of Universities and Colleges of Canada and Canadian Association of University Teachers, these actions have raised troubling concerns.

The All Chiefs' Task Force was mandated by the Chiefs of Saskatchewan in June 2005 to sort through the issues, and recommend how the First Nations University could best move forward into the future. Major findings included that the board of governors should be reduced in number and depoliticized, that academic freedom must be respected, and that the operations of the institution should be transparent. On May 30, 2006, Board Chair Watson responded by announcing the formation of a board that, while smaller at nineteen members, is in fact more political. Fifteen of the nineteen members are political representatives, and Mr. Watson continues as Board Chair, something the task force report had specifically recommended against. Former board members representing universities and governments have been removed from the board and assigned to a separate advisory committee. The same week, a report commissioned by the FNUC portrayed the Association of Universities and Colleges of Canada as having "non-interest and a lack of advocacy," something the AUCC quickly denied. The report concluded that FNUC should consider other routes of obtaining accreditation.[49]

The Association of Universities and Colleges of Canada announced in June 2006 that, for the first time in its ninety-year existence, it would set up a committee to review an institution's continued membership.[50] Whatever the outcome of this process will be, perhaps the lesson to be learned is that creating, operating, and maintaining an Aboriginal post-secondary institution within a colonialist environment that produces more failures than successes is a daunting challenge.

Conclusion

IN THE PROCESS OF CLAIMING SOVEREIGNTY over Canada, the British Crown assumed control over all the land and its resources in exchange for benefits that would be given to First Nations. The spirit of the treaties is such that First Nations were to receive something of significant value, and, in the case of the Numbered Treaties, this was largely represented by the demand for education that would enable future generations to share in the bounty of Canada. This access to opportunity extends to post-secondary education and implies that First Nations individuals should have unlimited access to any training for which they qualify. In addition, Aboriginal people should have the right to establish and control post-secondary institutions as a means of ensuring culturally appropriate and effective programs. Such a measure of compensation is modest indeed when compared to the value of resources from which Aboriginal peoples have been alienated. Given the removal of Aboriginal peoples from their original ownership of the vast resource wealth of the land, and lacking any major redirection of natural or financial resources, there exists, at the least, a moral justification for Canada to provide adequate funding for Aboriginal higher education.

The issue of jurisdiction over First Nations post-secondary education is complex and controversial. The federal government's current policy is to limit First Nations aspirations by delivering such education as a social program only in order to bring First Nations participation rates to a level comparable to the rest of society. The difficulty with such a strategy is that it does not deal directly with the notion of rights, and until this is done, perception will exist that government can arbitrarily cut funding at any time. The federal government must be explicit about its intentions by enacting legislation that will empower Aboriginal higher education institutions with the benefit of permanent funding. Canadians and their governments need to accept the notion that First Nations are a part of the national landscape, as are provinces and municipalities, and that Aboriginal citizens, treaty or otherwise, have legitimate entitlements to funded post-secondary education, both as individuals and in terms of controlling their own institutions.

Such unique collective rights are politically difficult to justify because they run counter to the liberal ideology of equal rights for all individuals, and, therefore, are highly unpopular for Parliament to entrench in legislation. However, the product of such a policy could be well-functioning Aboriginal communities with highly educated and motivated individuals who will be committed to, and play an important role in, contributing to the vision of the country. Being allowed to pursue this "new buffalo" will mean that future generations of Aboriginal peoples will not only have a special and unique ability to participate in post-secondary education, but will be able to acquire the tools that can one day enable them to contribute at the highest levels to the country they know as their homeland.

The challenges of finding more equitable means of delivering Aboriginal post-secondary education and of building Aboriginal self-government capacity will be a major test of governments' resolve to bring about major improvements in the lives of Aboriginal peoples.

Appendix A

Significant Dates Regarding First Nations Education

1876	Section 86(1) of *Indian Act:* Indians obtaining university degrees may be enfranchised.
1908	Indian Affairs provides the first assistance on a benevolent basis to an Indian to attend university.
1920	Scott attempts to introduce Bill 14 regarding compulsory enfranchisement.
1923	Emmanuel College closes.
1947	Joint Senate/House of Commons hearings foreshadow policy change.
1957	Indian Affairs introduces scholarships to assist Indians attending university.
1969	White Paper on Indian Policy advocates terminating Aboriginal and treaty rights. The first Native Studies program is established at Trent University.
1971	Funding for Cultural Education Centres is announced.
1973	Manitou Community College is established.
1975	Indian Affairs develops the E-12 Guidelines for post-secondary students.
1976	Saskatchewan Indian Federated College is established.

1977 Post-Secondary Education Assistance Program is announced.

1978 Joint Cabinet/National Indian Brotherhood Committee ceases.

1983 University and College Entrance Program is initiated.

1983–87 Constitutional conferences on Aboriginal Peoples.

1987 Capping of Indian post-secondary funding begins.

1988 Results of the Assembly of First Nations national consultations on education are released in the form of *Tradition and Education.* The Indian Studies Support Program is introduced.

1989 National Day of Protest against capping. The Post-Secondary Student Support Program is implemented.

1994 Indian Affairs begins to devolve post-secondary student funding
to bands and tribal councils.

1995 The Royal Commission on Aboriginal Peoples makes recommendations regarding Aboriginal higher education.

2000 The National Association of Indigenous Institutes of Higher Learning is formed.

2003 The most recent Indian Affairs policy review of First Nations higher education, the PSE Evaluation-Consolidated Report, is released.

Appendix B

Selected Institutions Receiving ISSP Funding (2001–2002)

British Columbia
   Chemainus Native College
   E'nowkin Centre
   Nicola Valley Institute of Technology

Alberta
   Blue Quills First Nations College
   Maskwachees Cultural College
   Old Sun Community College
   Red Crow Community College

Saskatchewan
   First Nations University of Canada
   Saskatchewan Indian Institute of Technologies

Manitoba
   Roseau River Tribal College
   West Region Tribal College
   Yellowquill College, Portage la Prairie
   Manitoba First Nations Post-Secondary Institute

Ontario
> Anishinabek Education Institute
> First Nations Technical Institute
> Lakehead University
> Nipissing University College
> Six Nations Polytechnic

Quebec
> Institute Culturel Educatif Montagnais
> University of Laval
> University of Ottawa

Atlantic Provinces
> Mikmaq Education Authority, NS
> Union of New Brunswick Indians, NB

Yukon
> Yukon College

Appendix C

Canadian Universities with Native Studies Degree Programs

University of British Columbia, Vancouver, BC (First Nations Studies)

University of Northern British Columbia, Prince George, BC (First Nations Studies)

University of Alberta, Edmonton, AB (School of Native Studies)

University of Lethbridge, Lethbridge, AB (Department of Native American Studies)

University of Regina/First Nations University of Canada, SK (Department of Indigenous Studies)

University of Saskatchewan, Saskatoon, SK (Department of Native Studies)

University of Manitoba, Winnipeg, MB (Department of Native Studies)

Brandon University, Brandon, MB (Department of Native Studies)

McMaster University, Hamilton, ON (Indigenous Studies)

Trent University, Peterborough, ON (Department of Native Studies)

University of Sudbury, Sudbury, ON (Native Studies Program)

St. Thomas University, Fredericton, NB (Department of Native Studies)

Appendix D

Recommendations of the Royal Commision on Aboriginal Peoples Regarding Post-Secondary Education

3.5.20

The government of Canada recognize and fulfil its obligation to treaty nations by supporting a full range of education services, including post-secondary education, for members of treaty nations where a promise of education appears in treaty texts, related documents or oral histories of the parties involved.

3.5.21

The federal government continue to support the costs of post-secondary education for First Nations and Inuit post-secondary students and make additional resources available

(a)   to mitigate the impact of increased costs as post-secondary institutions shift to a new policy environment in post-secondary education; and

(b)   to meet the anticipated higher level of demand for post-secondary education services.

3.5.22

A scholarship fund be established for Métis and other Aboriginal students who do not have access to financial support for post-secondary education under present policies, with

(a) lead financial support provided by federal and provincial governments and additional contributions from corporate and individual donors;

(b) a planning committee to be established immediately,

    (i) composed of Métis and other Aboriginal representatives, students, and federal and provincial representatives in balanced numbers;

    (ii) given a maximum two-year mandate; and

    (iii) charged with determining the appropriate vehicle, level of capitalization, program criteria and administrative structure for initiation and administration of the fund; and

(c) provisions for evaluating demand on the fund, its adequacy and its impact on participation and completion rates of Métis and other Aboriginal students in post-secondary studies.

3.5.23

Canada's post-secondary institutions recognize Aboriginal languages on a basis equal to other modern languages, for the purpose of granting credits for entrance requirements, fulfilment of second language requirements, and general course credits.

3.5.24

Public post-secondary institutions in the provinces and territories undertake new initiatives or extend current ones to increase the participation, retention and graduation of Aboriginal students by introducing, encouraging or enhancing

(a) a welcoming environment for Aboriginal students;

(b) Aboriginal content and perspectives in course offerings across disciplines;

(c) Aboriginal studies and programs as part of the institution's regular program offerings and included in the institution's core budget;

(d) Aboriginal appointments to boards of governors;

(e) Aboriginal councils to advise the president of the institution;

(f) active recruitment of Aboriginal students;

(g) admission policies that encourage access by Aboriginal applicants;

(h) meeting spaces for Aboriginal students;

(i) Aboriginal student unions;

(j) recruitment of Aboriginal faculty members;

(k) support services with Aboriginal counsellors for academic and personal counselling; and

(l) cross-cultural sensitivity training for faculty and staff.

3.5.25

Where there is Aboriginal support for an Aboriginal college within a university, and where numbers warrant, universities act to establish an Aboriginal college to serve as the focal point for the academic, residential, social and cultural lives of Aboriginal students on campus, and to promote Aboriginal scholarship.

3.5.26

Federal, provincial and territorial governments collaborate with Aboriginal governments and organizations to establish and support post-secondary educational institutions controlled by Aboriginal people, with negotiated allocation of responsibility for

(a)   core and program funding commensurate with the services they are expected to provide and comparable to the funding provided to provincial or territorial institutions delivering similar services;

(b)   planning, capital and start-up costs of new colleges and institutes;

(c)   improvement of facilities for community learning centres as required for new functions and development of new facilities where numbers warrant and the community establishes this as a priority; and

(d)   fulfilment of obligations pursuant to treaties and modern agreements with respect to education.

3.5.27

Aboriginally controlled post-secondary educational institutions collaborate to create regional boards and/or a Canada-wide board to

(a)   establish standards for accrediting programs provided by Aboriginal post-secondary institutions;

(b)   negotiate mutual recognition of course credits and credentials to facilitate student transfer between Aboriginal institutions and provincial and territorial post-secondary institutions;

(c)   establish co-operative working relationships with mainstream accreditation bodies such as the Association of Universities and Colleges of Canada and professional associations such as the Canadian Association of University Teachers; and

(d)   pursue other objectives related to the common interests of Aboriginal institutions.

Notes

INTRODUCTION

1. Ron Laliberte, Priscilla Settee et al., eds. *Expressions in Canadian Native Studies* (Saskatoon: University of Saskatchewan, 2000), x.

2. Michael Howlett, "Policy Paradigms and Policy Change: Lessons from the Old and New Canadian Policies Towards Aboriginal Peoples," *Policy Studies Journal* 22, 4 (1994): 631-649.

3. Linda Tuhiwai Smith, *Decolonizing Methodologies: Research and Indigenous Peoples* (New York: Zed Books, 1999), 28-32.

4. Ibid., 142-160.

5. Peter Hogg, *Constitutional Law in Canada* (Toronto: Carswell, 1998), 27-29.

6. Ibid.

7. Canadian Native Law Bulletin. (CNLB) [1978] No. 4, *Greyeyes v. The Queen,* reported (1978) 84 DLR (3d), 196.

8. For a list of policy studies, see Bibliography.

9. Winona Stevenson, "Prairie Indians and Higher Education: An Historical Overview 1876-1977," in *Hitting the Books,* ed. Terry Wotherspoon (Toronto: Garamond Press, 1991).

10. Ibid., 225-226.

11. Darlene Lanceley, "The Post-Secondary Assistance Program for Indian Education: The Vehicle for Change and the Voice of Opposition," in *Hitting the Books*, ed. Terry Wotherspoon (Toronto: Garamond Press, 1991).

12. For example, Ovide Mercredi, *In the Rapids* (Toronto: Penguin Books, 1993), and the *Report of the Royal Commission on Aboriginal Peoples.*

13. Assembly of First Nations, *Tradition and Education: Towards a Vision of Our Future* (Ottawa: Assembly of First Nations, 1988).

14. Royal Commission on Aboriginal Peoples, *Report of the Royal Commission on Aboriginal Peoples,* 5 vols. (Ottawa: Canada Communications Group, 1996).

CHAPTER ONE

1. Olive Dickason, *Canada's First Nations* (Don Mills: Oxford University Press, 2002), 264.

2. Herbert Spencer, "Progress: Its Law and Causes," *Westminster Review* 67 (April 1857): 445-64. See also M. Hawkes, *Social Darwinism in European and American Thought 1860-1945* (Cambridge: Cambridge University Press), 1997.

3. Reginald Horseman, *Race and Manifest Destiny: The Origins of American Racial Anglo-Saxonism* (Cambridge: Harvard University Press, 1981), 139.

4. Ibid., 142. The five main racial categories generally perceived by ethnologists were Caucasian, Ethiopian, Mongolian, Malayan, and American Indian.

5. Ibid., 143.

6. Ibid., 144-48.

7. Ibid., 146.

8. Ibid., 156-57.

9. Ibid., 150.

10. House of Commons, *Debates,* 46 Vict. (9 May 1883) 14: 1107-08.

11. Ibid., 1101.

12. Donald Creighton, *John A. Macdonald: The Old Chieftain* (Toronto: MacMillan, 1965), 352.

13. Dickason, *Canada's First Nations,* 225.

14. Ibid., 225.

15. Ibid., 232.

16. John Taylor, "The Development of an Indian Policy for the Canadian North-West, 1869-1879" (PhD thesis, Queen's University, 1975), 28.

17. Ibid., 19-21.

18. Ibid., 48.

19. Indian Claims Commission (ICC), *Roseau River Anishanabe First Nation Inquiry* (Ottawa: Indian Claims Commission, 2001), 21.

20. Ibid., 22

21. Ibid., 23.

22. Ibid., 26.

23. ICC, *Roseau River Inquiry,* 20.

24. Alexander Morris, *The Treaties of Canada with the Indians of Manitoba and the North-West Territories* (Toronto: Coles, 1979 reprint), 126-42.

25. ICC, *Roseau River Inquiry,* 32 and 51.

26. Morris, *The Treaties of Canada,* 62.

27. Ibid., 81. Morris uses the term "Indian country" here in recognition that it was unceded territory.

28. John Tobias, *The Government of Canada and the Ochapowace Band 1870-1933* (Regina: Federation of Saskatchewan Indians, 1973), 1-10. The reserves of Chacachas and Kakeeshiway, both original signatory chiefs, were amalgamated in 1881 to form Ochapowace Reserve.

29. Hugh Dempsey, *Big Bear, The End of Freedom* (Vancouver: Douglas and McIntyre, 1984), 74-75. Big Bear's desire to not be tethered to a reserve because of the treaty was misinterpreted as a fear of being hanged.

30. Ibid., 69.

31. The Blackfoot refer to themselves as *Siksika.*

32. Taylor, "The Development of an Indian Policy."

33. Arthur Ray, Jim Miller, and Frank Tough, *Bounty and Benevolence: A History of Saskatchewan Treaties* (Montreal: McGill-Queen's University Press, 2000).

34. Treaty Four Council of Chiefs, "Treaty Four First Nations Governance Model— History," Fort Qu'Appelle, October 2000, 2.

35. Marcel Swain, *Background Research for a Legal Opinion on Post-Secondary Education* (Ottawa: Assembly of First Nations, November 1991), 3.

36. Morris, *The Treaties of Canada,* 333.

37. Ibid., 96.

38. Sarah Carter, *Lost Harvests: Prairie Indian Reserve Farmers and Government Policy* (Montreal: McGill-Queen's University Press, 1990), 257. The Delga'amuth case recognized the validity of oral history in establishing Indian understandings of events.

39. Bob Beal and Rod Macleod, *Prairie Fire* (Edmonton: Hurtig, 1984), 75.

40. Douglas Leighton, "A Victorian Civil Servant at Work: Lawrence Vankoughnet and the Canadian Indian Department 1874-1893," in A. Getty and A. Lussier, *As Long as the Sun Shines and Waters Flow* (Vancouver: University of British Columbia Press, 1983), 106.

41. Beal and Mcleod, *Prairie Fire,* 29.

42. Blair Stonechild and Bill Waiser, *Loyal Till Death* (Calgary: Fifth House, 1997), 46.

43. NAC, Sir John A Macdonald Papers, vol. 107, J. Rae to Macdonald, 18 July 1884.

44. Dempsey, *Big Bear,* 139.

45. Beal and Macleod, *Prairie Fire,* 91.

46. Stonechild and Waiser, *Loyal Till Death,* 63.

47. Louis Riel, *The Complete Writings of Louis Riel* (Edmonton: University of Alberta, 1985), 372.

48. Stonechild and Waiser, *Loyal Till Death,* 205-59.

49. NAC, MG26, Dewdney Papers, 587–88, Macdonald to Dewdney, Nov. 20, 1885.

50. Canada, *Sessional Papers* (1886), *Annual Report of Indian Affairs,* 141.

51. NAC, RG10, vol. 3710. file 19, 550-3, Vankoughnet to Macdonald, August 17, 1885.

52. Dickason, *Canada's First Nations,* 230.

53. John Milloy, *A National Crime: The Canadian Government and the Residential School System 1879-1986* (Winnipeg: University of Manitoba, 1999), 23-31.

54. J. R. Miller, *Shingwauk's Vision: A History of Native Residential Schools* (Toronto: University of Toronto Press, 1996), 101-03. Lebret and Battleford are located in what is today Saskatchewan, and High River in what is now Alberta.

55. Milloy, *A National Crime,* 33-39, and Miller, *Shingwauk's Vision,* 124-27. Mandatory two-month summer holidays were not instituted by Indian Affairs until 1920.

56. Milloy, *A National Crime,* 67-71.

57. Miller, *Shingwuak's Vision,* 138-42.

58. Dickason., *Canada's First Nations,* 226.

59. RSC, *Indian Act* (1876), section 86(1).

60. Sharon Venne, *Indian Acts and Amendments, 1868-1975* (Saskatoon: Native Law Centre, 1981), 287.

61. Brian Titley, *A Narrow Vision: Duncan Campbell Scott and the Administration of Indian Affairs in Canada* (Vancouver: University of British Columbia Press, 1986), 49-50.

62. Ibid., 50.

63. Canada, *Sessional Papers, Annual Report of the Department of Indian Affairs* for the period ending March 31, 1928, Ottawa, 15. Annual reports for the 1920s indicated that all enfranchisements had occurred under this provision.

64. Titley, *A Narrow Vision,* 102.

65. Brian Titley, "The League of Indians of Canada: An Early Attempt to Create a National Native Organization," *Saskatchewan Indian Federated College Journal* 1, 1 (1984): 56.

66. D.C. Scott to J.P. Wright, 31 Dec. 1919, cited in Titley, "The League of Indians," 56.

67. D.C. Scott to Charles Stewart, 3 February 1922, cited in ibid., 58.

68. D.C. Scott to Sir James Loughheed, 21 February, 1921, cited in ibid., 57.

69. Ibid., 58.

70. John Leslie, "Assimilation, Integration or Termination? 1943-63," PhD thesis, Carleton University, 1999, 96.

71. Department of Indian Affairs, *Annual Report of the Department of Indian Affairs, 1925-26,* (Ottawa: The Author, 1926), 17.

72. Ibid., 14.

73. NAC, RG 10, vol. 3159, file 359, 506, A.O. Lamire to C. Cooke, Jan 8, 1902.

74. Ibid., Antoine Bastien to C. Cooke, 11 Jan. 1902.

75. Ibid., P. Picard to C. Cooke, 20 Jan. 1902.

76. Ibid., Picard to Cooke, 24 Jan. 24 1902.

77. Ibid., Daniel Lynch to C. Cooke, Jan. 14, 1902.

78. Ibid., Hill to Cooke, 18 Jan. 1902. According to Marsha Boulten, *Just a Minute More* (Toronto: McArthur and Co., 1999), 65-72, Oronhyatekha, reputed to be the first Indian medical doctor, was also a charming character. A large man with distinctive Indian features, he nevertheless managed to join several fraternal orders including the Orangemen, an organization open only to "white Christian males." He distinguished himself by becoming head of the Canadian branch of the International Order of Foresters [IOOF]). Under

Oronhyatekha's leadership, the IOOF became an international model of an association that provided excellent benefits to its members.

79. Ibid., Laird to Cooke, 10 Jan. 1902.
80. Ibid. According to Cooke's notes, the agent's name appears to be Sutherland, letter dated 10 Jan. 1902.
81. RG 10, vol. 3122, file 330,203, J. Jacobs to Secretary, Dept. of Indian Affairs, 30 June 1908.
82. Ibid., J. Jacobs to J.D. McLean, Secretary of Indian Affairs, 15 July 1908.
83. Ibid. J.D. McLean to J. Nicholson, Registrar, McGill University, 29 July 1908.
84. Ibid., M. Benson to D.C. Scott, 8 August 1908.
85. Ibid., J.D. McLean to W. Vaughn, McGill University, 10 May 1909.
86. Ibid., W. Vaughn to Secretary, Indian Affairs, 16 March 1910.
87. Ibid., Scott to Pedley, 14 June 1911.
88. Ibid., Jacobs to McLean, 10 July 1912.
89. Ibid., Jacobs to McLean, 26 Sept. 1913.
90. Ibid., Registrar's Office, McGill University, 22 April 1915.
91. Ibid., Jacobs to Scott. 28 Sept. 1915.
92. Ibid., S. Stewart, Assistant Secretary, to V. Vaughn, McGill University, 26 Oct. 1914.
93. Ibid., R.W. Lee to V. Vaughn, Registrar, McGill University, 14 June 1915.
94. Ibid., Festus Johnson to D.C. Scott, 16 Jan. 1917.
95. W.P. Thompson, *The University of Saskatchewan* (Toronto: University of Toronto Press, 1970), 3–5.
96. Ibid., 5-7.
97. NAC, RG 10, vol. 3932, file 117, 504-1, Assistant Indian Commissioner to Deputy Superintendent General, 21 June 1890.
98. Ibid., J.A. Mackay to Bishop of Saskatchewan and Calgary, 28 Sept. 1895.
99. Ibid. Memorandum, Benson to McLean, 10 May 1897.
101. Ibid., J. Taylor to T. Davis, 5 March 1901.
102. Ibid., Taylor to Davis, 20 March 1901.
103. Ibid., J. Taylor to Bishop of Saskatchewan, 26 Dec. 1901.

CHAPTER TWO

1. John Leslie, "Assimilation, Integration or Termination?: The Development of Canadian Indian Policy, 1943–1963," (PhD thesis, Carlton University, 1999), iv.
2. Ibid., 179.
3. Titley, *A Narrow Vision,* 22. Scott had a fifty-two-year career with Indian Affairs in Ottawa, and was Deputy Superintendent General of Indian Affairs from 1913 to 1932.
4. Leslie, "Assimilation," 67.

5. Ibid., 88-93. James Horton was Supreme Chief and John Tootoosis was Assistant Chief of the Indian Nation of North America.

6. Royal Commission on Aboriginal Peoples, *Report,* vol. 1, 297-99.

7. Denis Smith, *Rogue Tory: The Life and Legend of John G. Diefenbaker* (Toronto: MacFarlane, Walter and Ross, 1995), 224-27.

8. Laurie Barron, *Walking in Indian Moccasins* (Vancouver: University of British Columbia Press, 1997), 134.

9. James Pitsula, "The Saskatchewan CCF Government and Treaty Indians, 1944-64," *Canadian Historical Review* LXXV, 1 (1994): 30.

10. Ibid., 33.

11. Ibid., 49.

12. Dickason, *Canada's First Nations,* 305.

13. Sally Weaver, *Making Canadian Indian Policy: The Hidden Agenda* (Toronto: University of Toronto Press, 1981), 37-38.

14. Ibid., 20. The International Order of the Daughters of the Empire is a Canadian women's charitable organization formed in 1900. Its purpose was to promote patriotism, loyalty, and service, and members volunteer their time to improve the quality of life of others. The name was shortened to IODE in 1979.

15. Harry Hawthorn, et al., *A Survey of Contemporary Indians of Canada: Economic, Political, Educational Needs and Policies,* vol. 1 (Ottawa: Queen's Printer, 1966), 45.

16. Ibid., vol. 2, 39.

17. Ibid., vol. 2, 16 and 170.

18. Ibid., vol. 2, 168-73.

19. The phrase "Citizens Plus" would be used in the Alberta Indian Chiefs' response to the 1969 Indian policy.

20. Hawthorn, *A Survey,* vol. 2, 210.

21. Ibid., 7.

22. At $65 million, welfare was the second largest item in the Indian Affairs budget after education.

23. Weaver, *Making Candian Indian Policy,* 25-27.

24. Ibid., 28. George Manuel, Chief of the National Indian Brotherhood, got his start as a community development worker.

25. Harold Cardinal, *The Unjust Society* (Edmonton: Hurtig, 1969), 104.

26. Weaver, *Making Canadian Indian Policy,* 39.

27. Ibid., 40.

28. Ibid., 41.

29. Rick Ponting and Roger Gibbins, *Out of Irrelevance* (Scarborough: Butterworth and Company, 1980), 197. Wuttunee was ostracized by the Indian community in 1970 after he published his book *Ruffled Feathers,* which argued in favour of the 1969 Indian policy.

30. Palmer Patterson, *The Canadian Indian: A History Since 1500* (Don Mills: Collier-Macmillan, 1972), 177.

31. Dickason, *Canada's First Nations,* 361.

32. Ponting and Gibbins, *Out of Irrelevance,* 198; and Cardinal, *Unjust Society,* 170. Walter Dieter of Saskatchewan became the Brotherhood's first president.

33. Weaver, *Making Canadian Indian Policy,* 23 and 46. The "old boy network" had become so entrenched that Indian Affairs was derided as an embarrassing anomaly. When it was run military-style under Colonel Jones from 1953 to 1963, it was ridiculed as "Jones's lost battalion."

34. Ibid., 53-54. Trudeau referred to Indian desires to preserve their culture as the "wigwam complex."

35. "Trudeau: Handling of Indians Blot on Record," *Ottawa Citizen,* 13 June 1968.

36. Weaver, *Making Canadian Indian Policy,* 55.

37. Ibid., 60-61.

38. Ibid.

39. Ibid., 82. The conference was held at Glendon College in Toronto. The concept of Aboriginal rights was very recent, having just been introduced by the Nishga in their Supreme Court case was over land rights in the Nass Valley.

40. Ibid., 69-70.

41. Ibid., 90-96.

42. Ibid., 114.

43. Ibid., 169. A similar statement is contained in the text of the 1969 Indian Policy.

44. Cardinal, *Unjust Society,* 15.

45. "Alberta Indians Ready to Fight Federal Policy," *Globe and Mail,* 8 July 1969.

46. Weaver, *Making Canadian Indian Policy,* 179.

47. Harold Cardinal, *The Rebirth of Canada's Indians* (Edmonton: Hurtig, 1977), 164. Cardinal maintains that Barber's open-mindedness in looking at Indian Claims outside the narrow mandate of the commission was helpful in opening the mind of the federal government about Aboriginal rights and comprehensive land claims.

48. Indian Chiefs of Alberta, *Citizens Plus* (Edmonton: Indian Association of Alberta, 1970), 4.

49. Statement by Prime Minister Trudeau at a meeting with the Indian Association of Alberta, Ottawa, June 4, 1970 cited in Weaver, *Making Canadian Indian Policy,* 185.

50. Milloy, *National Crime,* 203.

51. Federation of Saskatchewan Indians, *Indian Education in Saskatchewan,* 3 vols. (Saskatoon: Saskatchewan Indian Cultural College, 1973), 149.

52. Ibid., 279.

53. Ibid., 233-36.

54. Jean Barman, Yvonne Hebert, and Don McCaskill, *Indian Education in Canada: The Legacy* (Vancouver: University of British Columbia Press, 1986), 150-69.

55. Diefenbaker recalled that once, in his childhood, armed Indians appeared at his family's door to warn them about a mentally disturbed Indian who was in the area. The youthful Diefenbaker interpreted this as Indians protecting his family. Personal communication with Bruce Sheppard, Director, Diefenbaker Centre, 24 Oct. 2003.

56. Department of Indian Affairs, *Annual Report, 1957-58,* 60.

57. Department of Indian Affairs, *Annual Report, 1963-64,* 25.

58. Department of Indian Affairs, *Annual Report, 1957-58,* 59.

59. Department of Indian Affairs, *Annual Report, 1960-61,* 57.

60. Indian and Eskimo Affairs Program, *The Indian and Inuit Graduate Register 1976* (Ottawa: Indian and Northern Affairs, 1977).

61. Ibid.

CHAPTER THREE

1. Margaret Ward, "Indian Education in Canada: Implementation of Indian Policy, 1973-1978," (MEd thesis, University of Saskatchewan, 1988), 14.

2. Cardinal, *Rebirth,* 113-14. The *Indian Act* revision was partly in response to troublesome court challenges such as the Lavell case. Indian groups, in particular the Federation of Saskatchewan Indians, promoted the "Principles of Indian Government" as a counterpoint to the devolution policy.

3. Ponting and Gibbons, *Out of Irrelevance,* 221-23.

4. House of Commons, Standing Committee on Indian Affairs and Northern Development, *Minutes of Procedings and Evidence,* 24 May 1973, issue 18, 7.

5. Royal Commission on Aboriginal Peoples, *Report,* vol. 2 (Ottawa: Canada Communications Group, 1995), 535. The James Bay Settlement of 1975 included a cash payment of $232 million, interest in 68,000 square kilometres of land, and control over local affairs.

6. Dickason, *Canada's First Nations,* 305-07. The Drybones case established that Indians had a right to consume alcohol as did other citizens.

7. Cardinal, *Rebirth,* 110-12, and Weaver, *Making Canadian Indian Policy,* 199.

8. Don Purich, *Our Land, Native Rights in Canada* (Toronto: Lorimer, 1986), 184. It was rumoured that infiltrators from the Communist Party had been responsible for inciting the violence.

9. Dickason, *Canada's First Nations,* 363.

10. House of Commons, *Debates,* 24 Oct. 1974, 746.

11. Cardinal, *Rebirth,* 115.

12. Barber Papers 81-12, "The Joint Cabinet/NIB Committee Structure," Regina: University of Regina Archives.

13. Ponting and Gibbins, *Out of Irrelevance,* 258, and Cardinal, *Rebirth,* 185. Cardinal maintains that Trudeau made a commitment, at the 1970 Cabinet meeting where the Red Paper was presented, to have regular meetings between Cabinet and the Brotherhood, but a lack of follow-up caused the idea to die. National Indian Brotherhood Vice-President Clive Linklater, who was handling the fallout from the Parliament Hill confrontation, revived the idea. When Indian Affairs Minister Judd Buchanan spurned the idea, Linklater appealed to John Turner and Jean Chretien to intervene on the behalf of the NIB. Although Buchanan still rejected the idea, Linklater gambled by stating in a press conference that Cabinet would meet with the Brotherhood. The ruse worked and the meeting occurred.

14. Ponting and Gibbins, *Out of Irrelevance,* 147 and 151, and Weaver, *Making Canadian Indian Policy,* 203. Cardinal's term as Regional Director General for the Alberta region was short and controversial. He thought that he had unqualified support from his superiors for radical change. He moved six senior officials into basement offices and brought in Indian consultants, some of whom had connections to the American Indian Movement. His actions alienated departmental staff, but he also managed to reveal mismanagement of departmental funding. Ahab Spence, at age sixty-five, was hired as a special advisor to Cam Mackie.

15. Sally Weaver, "The Joint Cabinet/National Indian Brotherhood Committee," *Canadian Public Administration* 25 (Summer 1982): 214.

16. "Chronology of the National Indian Brotherhood Education Program, 1976–1977" (unpublished, nd) cited in Ward, *Indian Education in Canada,* 102.

17. Joint Cabinet/National Indian Brotherhood Sub-Committee, "Verbatim Minutes of Meeting on 27 June 1977," 7, in Ward, *Indian Education in Canada,* 109.

18. Ward, *Indian Education in Canada,* 9.

19. Cardinal, *Rebirth,* 114.

20. Ward, *Indian Education in Canada,* 84–85.

21. Indian Association of Alberta, Indian Act Study Team, "Proposed Revisions to the Indian Act," 6 August 1974, section 360.

22. Joint Cabinet/National Indian Brotherhood Committee, "Verbatim Minutes of Meeting, 11 July 1977," records of National Indian Brotherhood, Ottawa, cited in Ward, *Indian Education in Canada,* 110.

23. Ward, *Indian Education in Canada,* 123.

24. Canadian Indian Rights Commission, "Summary Minutes of the Joint Committee of Cabinet and the National Indian Brotherhood Meeting of 12 December 1977," 10–13, in Ward, *Indian Education in Canada,* 126–27.

25. National Indian Brotherhood, *Indian Control of Indian Education* (Ottawa: National Indian Brotherhood, 1972), 3.

26. Ponting and Gibbins, *Out of Irrelevance,* 259, and Cardinal, *Rebirth,* 165. Improved relations helped the NIB reach an agreement in 1975 over land claims processes.

27. Ward, *Indian Education in Canada,* 130.

28. Joint Cabinet/National Indian Brotherhood Committee, "Verbatim Minutes of Meeting on 11 July 1977," 3, cited in Ward, *Indian Education in Canada,* 131.

29. National Indian Brotherhood, *Indian Control of Indian Education* (Ottawa: The Author, 1972), 16.

30. Saskatchewan Indian Cultural College, "A Commentary on the History of Cultural-Educational Centres Funding," Saskatoon (unpublished paper, nd), 1.

31. Author's personal collection, *Progress Report of Manitou Community College,* Nov. 1973–Aug. 1974."

32. Cardinal, *Unjust Society,* 187.

33. House of Commons Standing Committee on Indian Affairs and Northern Development, *Minutes of Proceedings and Evidence,* 24 May 1973, no. 18, 9.

34. House of Commons, Standing Committee on Indian Affairs and Northern Development, *Minutes of Proceedings and Evidence,* 22 May 1973, issue 17, 11.

35. Evalucan Ltd., *Evaluation of the Cultural/Educational Centres Programme* (Calgary: Evalucan 1978), 104.

36. Ward, *Indian Education in Canada,* 52–53 and 72–73.

37. Ibid., 54.

38. Aboriginal Institute of Canada, "A Case Study of 'Flim Flam' or 'Now You See it, Now You Don't': The 42 Million Dollar Cultural Education Program," Ottawa, 5 Feb. 1976, 4–5.

39. Ibid., 5–6.

40. Saskatchewan Indian Cultural College, "A Commentary," 15.

41. Gail Valaskakis, interview, 18 April 2002, Ottawa.

42. Author's personal collection, Indian Affairs, Working Committee on Manitou College, Feb. 18–19 minutes. Native students of the McGill Intertribal Council and faculty at McGill and other Montreal-area post-secondary institutions established the Native North American Studies Institute in 1971. The board was comprised of four professors, four students, three representatives of the Indians of Quebec Association, and one from the Northern Quebec Inuit Association. The Institute received a McConnell Foundation Grant of $17,000, and hired an American citizen, G. William Craig, as General Director.

43. In 1958, when the Diefenbaker government concluded that it was not feasible to manufacture the AVRO Arrow, part of the agreed-upon resolution was the establishment of two Bomarc missile bases as a Cold War deterrent. The Americans built one at North Bay, the other at La Macaza, Quebec.

44. Treaties and Historical Centre, file 1/25-22-30, vol. 30, Acceptance of Offer, Crown Assets Corporation, Indian and Northern Affairs, Ottawa, 11 January 1973. Treasury Board Minute 716204.

45. Gail Valaskakis, interview, Ottawa, 18 April 2002.

46. Treaties and Historical Centre, File 1/25-22-30, vol. 30, Proposal, Treasury Board Minute 716204 (nd).

47. CEGEP is the Quebec two-year program that was the equivalent of what was Grade 13 and first year university in Ontario.

48. Author's personal collection, Manitou College, *Progress Report*, 15 Nov. 1973, to 15 Aug. 1974, 9.

49. Author's personal collection, Manitou Community College, *Status Report to Assistant Deputy Minister of Indian Affairs*, 14 Dec. 1973, 2.

50. Author's personal collection, W. Cisneros, *Native Education in Quebec: A Report to the Challenge for Change Division of the National Film Board*, nd.

51. Author's personal collection, Manitou Community College, Calendar 1974–1975. Choices in physical education included hockey, skiing, basketball, gymnastics, volleyball, swimming, and bowling.

52. Author's personal collection, Manitou College, *Academic Report*, 9 Oct. 1974, 2.

53. Author's personal collection, Manitou College, *Progress Report*, 15 Nov. 1973, to 15 Aug. 1974, 8.

54. Author's personal collection, Manitou College, *Academic Report*, 21 March 1975, 1.

55. Native North American Studies Institute, *The First Peoples in Quebec*, vol. 2, 163.

56. Manitou Community College, *Progress Report* to 15 Aug. 1974, 8.

57. Ibid., 11.

58. Ibid., 13.

59. Manitou Community College, *Progress Report* to 15 Aug. 1974.

60. Author's personal collection, Native North American Studies Institute Board of Directors, Minutes, 9 Nov. 1973. George Miller was a member of the Six Nations reserve, and a graduate student at Stanford University at the time.

61. Manitou Community College, *Status Report*, 6.

62. Author's personal collection, Manitou College, *Financial Report to the Indians of Quebec Association*, 23 Aug. 1974, 1.

63. Ibid., 5.

64. Manitou Community College, *Progress Report* to 15 Aug. 1974, 18.

65. Author's personal collection, Manitou College, *Progress Report*, 15 Nov. 1973 to 15 Aug. 1974, 20.

66. Ibid., 22.

67. Ibid., 2.

68. Ibid., 3.

69. The teacher training program at Manitou College preceded the establishment of the Northern Teacher Education Program (NORTEP) created in 1977 and the Saskatchewan Urban Teacher Education Program (SUNTEP) founded in 1980.

70. Author's personal collection, Manitou Community College Board of Governors, Minutes, 18 Feb. 1975, 19.

71. Ibid., *Recruiting Report for Ontario*, 21-29 Nov. 1974 by recruiter Blair Stonechild.

72. Ibid., Joanne Reyome, "As I See It," letter, nd.

73. Indian and Northern Affairs, Treaties and Historical Research Centre, Hull, file 1/25-22-30, vol. 30, Assistant Deputy Minister Mackie to Chief P. Pietacho, 26 Jan. 1976.

74. Ibid., George Manuel to Judd Buchanan, Minister, Indian Affairs, 11 Feb. 1976.

75. Ibid., Claude Rabeau to Minister Buchanan, 19 Feb. 1976 (translated from French).

76. Ibid., Oka Indian Office, Band Council Resolution #84-75/76, 20 Feb. 1976.

77. Ibid., file 1/25-22-30, George Miller to Local 10924, Public Service Alliance of Canada, 26 April 1976.

78. Ibid. Senator Guy Williams to Judd Buchanan, 20 May 1976.

79. Ibid., Judd Buchanan to Hon. G. Williams, 10 Aug. 1976.

80. Ibid., file 1/25-22-30, vol. 30, E.T. Parker, Director of Finance and Management, Indian and Eskimo Affairs, Ottawa, 25 Aug. 1976.

81. Ibid., file 1/25-22-30, vol. 31, Minutes, Board of Governors Meeting, Manitou College, 4 Dec. 1976, Montreal.

82. Ibid.

83. Ibid., file 1/25-22-30, vol. 31, Update of Minister's briefing cards on Manitou Community College—Closing of Manitou College's Operations at La Macaza, nd.

84. Ibid., R. Connelly to P. Mackie, Indian Affairs, Ottawa, 23 Dec. 1976.

85. Gail Valaskakis, Interview, Ottawa, 18 April 2002.

86. NIB, *Indian Control of Indian Education* (Ottawa: The Author, 1982), 3 and 14.

87. Ward, *Indian Education in Canada,* 21. A national Indian higher education student association called the National Native Student Association had been funded by the Secretary of State in 1971. By 1971 the organization had been renamed the Native Youth Association of Canada. It formed provincial wings and had a head office in Ottawa. The association ceased operations in 1976. Presidents included Edith Whetung, Blair Stonechild, and Arthur Manuel. Peter McFarlane's *Brotherhood to Nationhood,* 186, describes some of the association's activities.

88. Ibid., 216-18.

89. Indian and Northern Affairs Canada, "Historical Evolution of the Post-Secondary Education Program" (Ottawa: The Author, nd).

90. Indian and Northern Affairs Canada, "Post-Secondary Education for Status Indians and Inuit" (Ottawa: The Author, 1997), 1.

91. Darlene Lanceley, "The Post-Secondary Assistance Program for Indian Education: The Vehicle for Change and the Voice of Opposition," in Terry Wotherspoon, *Hitting the Books* (Toronto: Garamond Press, 1991), 241-42.

92. Ward, *Indian Education in Canada,* 220-24.

93. Ibid., 41. The number of students reported by Ward is about 1500 lower than the 4148 reported by Indian Affairs for 1978-79.

94. Stevenson, "Prairie Indians and Higher Education," in Wotherspoon, *Hitting the Books,* 229.

95. Indian and Northern Affairs Canada, *Executive Summary: Post-Secondary Education Assistance Evaluation Study* (Ottawa: Evaluation Branch, 1985), 5.

96. Ibid., 7.

97. Ibid., 10.

98. Blair Stonechild and Don McCaskill, "The Development of Indian/Native Studies in Canada," in *Education, Research, Information Systems and the North,* ed. Peter Adams (Ottawa: Association of Universities for Northern Studies, 1987), 103-04.

99. Ibid., 104.

100. Joseph Couture, "Native Studies and the Academy," in G. Sefa Dei, B. Hall, and D. Rosenberg, eds, *Indigenous Knowledges in Global Contexts* (Toronto: University of Toronto, 2000), 157-67. Similar sentiments are expressed in Peter Kulchyski's "What is Native Studies" and Neal McLeod's "Indigenous Studies: Negotiating the Space Between Tribal Communities and Academia," in Ron Laliberte, Priscilla Settee, et al., *Expressions in Canadian Native Studies* (Saskatoon: University of Saskatchewan, 2000), 27-39.

101. Elizabeth Cook-Lynn, "American Indian Intellectualism and the New Indian Story," in *Natives and Academics: Researching and Writing about American Indians,* ed. Mihesuah, Devon (Lincoln: University of Nebraska Press, 1998), 112 and 126.

102. Verna Kirkness, "Native Teachers: A Key to Progress," *Canadian Journal of Native Education* 13 (1986): 48.

103. Donald Taylor, Martha Crago, and Lynne Alpine, "Education in Aboriginal Communities: Dilemmas around Empowerment," *Canadian Journal of Native Education* 20 (1993).

104. Alaska Native Knowledge Network, "Who is this child named WIPCE [World Indigenous Peoples Conference on Education]," *Sharing Our Pathways* 7, 4 (2002): 3.

105. "Indians and the University," *The Green and White: The University of Saskatchewan Alumni Association Magazine* (Winter 1973): 9. Renaud hoped that the college, now known as the Saskatchewan Indian Cultural Centre, would become affiliated with the university.

106. Ibid., 12.

107. G.S. Basran, "History and Rationale of the Affirmative Action Program, College of Arts and Science, University of Saskatchewan," *Canadian Journal of Native Studies* X, 2 (1990): 280-82.

108. Ibid., 283-87.

109. Stonechild and McCaskill, "The Development of Indian/Native Studies," 5.

110. Marie Battiste, *Post-Colonial Project Description,* at <www.usask.ca/education/postcolonial/description.htm>.

111. Shona Taner, "The Development of Native Studies at Canadian Universities: Four Programs, Four Provinces Four Decades," master's thesis, Carleton University, 1997, 109. The Native Studies programs studied were at Trent University, University of Alberta, University of Northern British Columbia, and the Saskatchewan Indian Federated College at the University of Regina.

112. Blair Stonechild, "A History of Canadian/Native Studies Association (CINSA)," unpublished paper, Saskatchewan Indian Federated College, Regina, 2001, 1-2.

113. Blair Stonechild, President, CINSA letter to Paule Leduc, President, Social Sciences and Humanities Research Council of Canada, 7 July 1988, SIFC Archives, Regina.

114. Mihesuah, *Natives and Academics,* 66.

115. Royal Commission on Aboriginal Peoples, *Report,* vol. 3 (Ottawa: Canada Communications Group, 1996), 514-16.

116. Ibid., 515-17.

CHAPTER FOUR

1. Assembly of First Nations, *Tradition and Education: Towards a Vision of Our Future,* vol. 1 (Ottawa: Assembly of First Nations, 1989).

2. Sally Weaver, *Making Canadian Indian Policy* (Toronto: University of Toronto Press, 1981), 14.

3. J.R. Miller, *Skyscrapers Hide the Heavens* (Toronto: University of Toronto, 1989), 238; and Ponting and Gibbins, *Out of Irrelevance,* 213. The Indians had accepted observer status at the 1978 First Ministers' Conference on the constitution but had obviously been dissatisfied with the arrangement.

4. Norma Sluman and Jean Goodwill, *John Tootoosis* (Ottawa: Golden Dog Press, 1982), 229.

5. Ibid., 231. John Tootoosis, subject of the book, was a member of the delegation. An estimated 120 interviews were conducted with journalists from around the world.

6. Miller, *Skyscrapers,* 238; and Ponting and Gibbins, *Out of Irrelevance,* 214. Clark offered to hold a two-day meeting of Cabinet and the governor general in an effort to dissuade Indian leaders from travelling to England. This offer was rejected.

7. Miller, *Skyscrapers,* 239.

8. Sluman and Goodwill, *John Tootoosis,* 232.

9. Ibid., 232; and Ponting and Gibbins, *Out of Irrelevance,* 214. The Pepin-Robarts Task Force on Unity recommendation that Indians be included in constitutional negotiations also placed pressure on Trudeau.

10. Miller, *Skyscrapers,* 239.

11. Ibid. Also excluded were references to women's rights.

12. Sluman and Goodwill, *John Tootoosis,* 234, and *Report of the Royal Commission on Aboriginal Peoples,* vol. 1, 207.

13. Ibid., 235.

14. Ibid.

15. Canada, *Constitution Act,* 1982.

16. Miller, *Skyscrapers,* 244–45.

17. Sally Weaver, "Indian Policy in the New Conservative Government, Part 1: The Nielsen Task Force of 1985," *Native Studies Review* 2, 1 (1986): 12.

18. Ibid., 15.

19. "Ottawa's Assault on First Nations Education," *Saskatchewan Indian* (April 1989): 6.

20. Weaver, "Indian Policy," 22–28.

21. INAC, Treaties and Historical Centre, file A119725, Penner, Keith, Opposition Critic for Indian Affairs to Hon. William McKnight, Minister of Indian Affairs, House of Commons, Ottawa, 22 Jan. 1987.

22. Ibid., file A175137, Schulze, David, Post-Graduate Students' Society of McGill University to Hon. Bill McKnight, Minister for Indian and Northern Affairs, Montreal, 2 Mar. 1987.

23. Ibid., file A126715, Peters, Gordon, Ontario Regional Chief to Hon. William McKnight, Minister, Indian and Northern Affairs Canada, Toronto, 16 Mar. 1987.

24. Ibid., Briefing for Deputy Minister, Originator: D. Wattie, Treaties and Historical Research Centre, Indian and Northern Affairs, Gatineau, 31 Mar. 1987.

25. INAC, Briefing for the Minister, Treaties and Historical Centre, Gatineau, file E-4727-1, 15 Apr.1987.

26. Treaties and Historical Centre, file A126715, Briefing for the Minister, Revisions to existing E-12 guidelines, 15 Apr. 1987.

27. Treaties and Historical Centre, NARC 5-119, box 2, Bill McKnight to Chief and Council, 12 May 1987.

28. "Cutbacks Hit Hard on Post-secondary Students," *Saskatchewan Indian* (Fall 1987): 8.

29. "Indian Students Protest Capped Educational Funding," *Saskatchewan Indian* (Sept. 1988): 17.

30. Treaties and Historical Centre, file A12675a, Parry, John to Hon. Bill McKnight, Ottawa, 21 May 1987. A copy was forwarded to all Members of Parliament.

31. Treaties and Historical Centre, Gatineau, file A147452, Minister of Indian Affairs to President, Canadian Association of University Teachers, Ottawa, 27 Oct. 1987.

32. Ibid., "Press Line: Student Assistance Program" (nd).

33. Ibid. Fifteen thousand American Indian students received a total of USD $39.2 million in scholarship grants from the Bureau of Indian Affairs, compared to a total of $130 million in Canada for Indian post-secondary education in 1988.

34. *Report of the Auditor General for the Period Ending March 31, 1986,* Ottawa, Items 11.73 and 11.76.

35. *Report of the Auditor General for the Period Ending March 31, 1988,* Ottawa, Item 14.44.

36. Ibid., Item 14.41.

37. Ibid., Item 14.53.

38. Treaties and Historical Centre, File A153805, Hon. Bill McKnight to Chief and Council, Treaties and Historical Centre, Indian and Northern Affairs, Gatineau, 30 May 1988.

39. Assembly of First Nations, *Tradition and Education: Towards a Vision of Our Future,* vol. 1 (Ottawa: Assembly of First Nations, 1988), 92–93 and 97.

40. Ibid., 96–99.

41. National Indian Education Forum (NIEF) and Alexander School Board, *Interim Recommended Changes to the Post-Secondary Student Assistance Program,* (Morinville, Alberta: August 18, 1989), 4.

42. Jeremy Hull, *An Overview of the Educational Characteristics of Registered Indians in Canada* (Ottawa: Indian and Northern Affairs Canada, 1987), xxii.

43. NIEF, *Interim Recommended Changes,* 6 and 11.

44. Treaties and Historical Centre, File N145123, Press Line, 18 Oct. 1988, Treaties and Historical Research Centre, Indian and Northern Affairs, Gatineau.

45. Ibid.

46. Treaties and Historical Centre, File K217163, Director General, Communications Branch to Deputy Minister, 5 June 1989, Treaties and Historical Research Centre, Gatineau. The Department of Indian Affairs and Federation of Saskatchewan Indian Nations had agreed to establish a Joint Working Group to address the issue of giving First Nations students full accessibility to post-secondary funding.

47. "Ottawa's Assault on First Nations Education," *Saskatchewan Indian* (April 1989).

48. Treaties and Historical Centre, File K217163, Communiqué, Minister of Indian Affairs and Northern Development, "New Policy on the Post-Secondary Student Assistance Program," 20 Mar. 1989.

49. House of Commons, Standing Committee on Aboriginal Affairs, *A Review of the Post-Secondary Student Assistance Program of the Department of Indian Affairs and Northern Development* (Ottawa: The Author, 1989).

50. Ibid., 38–41.

51. Ibid., 28.

52. Ibid., 35.

53. Ibid., 55.

54. Ibid., 61.

55. CNLB [1978] No.4, *Greyeyes v. The Queen,* Reported (1978) 84 D.L.R. (3d) 196.

56. Assembly of First Nations, 10th Annual Chiefs Assembly, Quebec City, Resolution No. 7/89.

57. NIEF, *Interim Recommended Changes,* 16.

58. "Ottawa's Assault on on First Nations Education," *Saskatchewan Indian* (April 1989): 6.

59. FSIN-DIAND Policy Review and Change Working Group, *Preliminary Investigation Report: Immediate Changes Required to the* DIAND'S *Post-secondary Student Assistance Program* (Ottawa: The Author, no date), ii.

60. "Implications for Indian Post-Secondary Education: The SIFC Response," SIFC *Journal* 4, 2 (1988): 5-15.

61. Treaties and Historical Research Centre, Gatineau, file A4727-1, Minister of Indian Affairs Pierre Cadieux to Chiefs and Council, 12 Sept. 1989.

62. Evaluation Directorate, *Evaluation of the Post-Secondary Education Assistance Program, Summary Report* (Ottawa: Indian and Northern Affairs, 1989), 1-2.

63. Ibid., 5.

64. Complied from: Standing Committee on Indian Affairs, 1989, 39; INAC, *Basic Departmental Data* ; Standing Committee on Aboriginal Affairs, 1990, 27:33; and DIAND 1987-88 Estimates, Part III, 2-67.

65. Standing Committee (1990), 8.

66. Ibid., 14-15.

67. Ibid., 7-13.

68. Indian and Northern Affairs Canada, Information Sheet No. 5, July 1989.

69. Standing Committee (1990), 15-17.

70. The Federation of Saskatchewan Indians was renamed the Federation of Saskatchewan Indian Nations (FSIN) after the signing of a political convention in 1982.

71. "Saskatchewan Indian Cultural College and University of Saskatchewan Affiliation," January 1974, Blakeney Papers GR 238, file R565.

72. Saskatchewan Archives, Blakeney Papers, MacMurchy to Ahenakew, 10 Jan. 1975, GR238, file R565.

73. Blakeney Papers, MacMurchy to Blakeney, 21 Nov. 1974, GR238, file R565.

74. Ibid., "Agenda Notes—Meeting with the Premier," nd, GR238, file R565.

75. Ibid., R565, vii-110(f), Ahenakew to Blakeney, 2 Nov. 1976.

76. John R. McLeod personal papers held by Neal McLeod, First Nations University of Canada.

77. Saskatchewan Indian Federated College (SIFC), "Briefing Notes for Meeting with the Cabinet, Government of Saskatchewan, January 31, 1997—SIFC's growth 1976-1995," Regina.

78. Dr. Barber had resigned as vice-president at the University of Saskatchewan in early 1974, just before a proposal by the Federation of Saskatchewan Indians for an Indian-controlled college was made to that university in

1975. The University of Regina became independent from the University of Saskatchewan in 1974 and Dr. Barber became its president in 1976.

79.   For a history of early development of federated colleges in Saskatchewan, see A. de Valk, "Independent University or Federated College?" *Saskatchewan History* XXX (1977).

80.   "The mission of the Saskatchewan Indian Federated College is to enhance the quality of life, and to preserve, protect and interpret the history, language, culture and artistic heritage of First Nations. The College will acquire and expand its base of knowledge and understanding in the best interests of First Nations and for the benefit of society by providing opportunities of quality bilingual and bi cultural education under the mandate and control of the First Nations of Saskatchewan. The SIFC is a First Nations controlled university college, which provides educational opportunities to both First Nations and non-First Nations students, selected from a provincial, national and international base." (Saskatchewan Indian Federated College Academic Calendar, 1998-2000, p. 1.)

81   "SIFC History," in SIFC Academic Calendar, 1999-2000.

82.   Blakeney Papers, R565, vii–110(f), MacMurchy to Ahenakew, 16 Dec. 1976.

83.   Ibid., R565, vii–110(f), Chief David Ahenakew, Address to the FSI Annual Conference, 12-14 Oct. 1976, 10.

84.   Ibid., R565, vii–110(f), Faris to Ahenakew, 29 Nov. 1976.

85.   Ibid., R565, vii–110(h), Remarks for a meeting..., 18 July 1977.

86.   Ibid..

87.   Ibid., Ahenakew to Faulkner, 9 Nov. 1977.

88.   Ibid., Special Assistant Norton to the Premier, 13 Dec. 1977.

89.   Ibid., follow-up to July 18 FSI/Cabinet meeting, 21 Oct. 1977.

90.   Ibid., MacMurchy to Ahenakew, 5 Sept. 1978.

91.   Blakeney Papers, R800, xliii, 64a(1) document 1-7835, 21 Sept. 1978.

92.   Ibid., Sanderson to Faris, 1 Aug. 1978.

93.   Ibid., Notes of FSI/Cabinet meeting, 20 Dec. 1979.

94.   Blakeney Papers, R800, xliii, 64a(3), MacMurchy to Sanderson, 28 Oct. 1980. Ahenakew assisted Munro during the 1984 federal election.

95.   Assembly of First Nations, *Tradition and Education,* 62-65.

96.   Anaquod, Del and Donna Pinay, "An Historical Overview of the Saskatchewan Indian Federated College: 1976-1998," unpublished document, Saskatchewan Indian Federated College, Regina, Nov. 1998.

97.   The urban Aboriginal population in Saskatoon would be comparable to that of Regina at approximately 20,000. The high proportion of Aboriginal people in and around Prince Albert led the chiefs of the area to request the establishment of a northern campus. In 1996, there were 610 students enrolled in Regina, 402 in Saskatoon, and 229 off-campus.

CHAPTER FIVE

1. Menno Boldt, *Surviving as Indians: The Challenge of Self-Government* (Toronto: University of Toronto Press, 1993), 128–29.

2. Cairns, *Citizens Plus,* 211–12.

3. Rand Dyck, *Canadian Politics: Critical Approaches,* 2nd ed. (Toronto: Nelson Canada, 1996), 626.

4. Tom Flanagan, *First Nations, Second Thoughts* (Montreal: McGill-Queen's University Press, 2000), 60–66.

5. Ibid., 110–11.

6. Government of Canada, Privy Council Office, *Consensus Report on the Constitution,* 28 Aug. 1992.

7. Special Committee on Self-Government, *Report of the Special Committee on Indian Self-Government in Canada* (Ottawa: House of Commons, Ottawa, 1983) 141–46.

8. Royal Commission on Aboriginal Peoples (RCAP), *Report,* vol. 5, 5.

9. Ibid., 5.

10. *Webster's University Dictionary* (Boston: Houghton-Mifflin, 1988).

11. Cairns, *Citizens Plus,* 113.

12. Government of Canada, *Federal Policy Guide: Aboriginal Self-Government* (Ottawa: Indian Affairs and Northern Development, 1995).

13. Cairns, *Citizens Plus,* 197.

14. Dickason, *Canada's First Nations,* 408–09.

15. RCAP, *Report,* vol. 3, 519–22.

16. Ibid., 506–07.

17. On 21 June 2003, the Saskatchewan Indian Federated College was renamed First Nations University of Canada.

18. RCAP, *Report,* vol. 3, 517–19.

19. Marie Battiste and Jean Barman, *First Nations Education in Canada: The Circle Unfolds* (Vancouver: University of British Columbia Press, 1995), vii–xix.

20. Ibid., 520–21.

21. RCAP, *Report,* vol. 3, 530–32.

22. Eber Hampton and Steve Wolfson, "Education for Self-Determination," in Hylton, J., *Aboriginal Self-Government in Canada* (Saskatoon: Purich Publishing, 1999), 93.

23. Ibid., 94–102.

24. Ray Barnhardt, "Higher Education in the Fourth World: Indigenous People Take Control," *Canadian Journal of Native Education* 18, 2 (1991): 6.

25. Ibid.

26. Ibid.

27. Indian Affairs and Northern Development, "Indian Studies Support Program" (Ottawa: The Author, 1990), 2.

28. Ibid., 1.

29. Indian Governments of Saskatchewan, *An Act Respecting the Saskatchewan Indian Federated College,* 26 May 1994, 3.

30. Stuart Smith, *Report of Commission of Inquiry on Canadian University Education* (Ottawa: Association of Universities and Colleges of Canada, 1991), 97-99.

31. "SIFC's Changing Relationships," in *Briefing Notes for Meeting with the Cabinet,* Government of Saskatchewan, 31 Jan. 1997.

32. Ibid., 6.

33. Ibid., "Study of SIFC Student Enrollment by Indian Status, Fall 1994."

34. Ibid., "SIFC's Changing Relationships," 5.

35. Ibid., "SIFC's Growth 1976-1995," 1-4.

36. Eber Hampton, "First Nations-Controlled University Education in Canada," in M. Castellano, L. Davis, and L. Lahache, *Aboriginal Education: Fulfilling the Promise* (Vancouver: University of British Columbia Press, 2000), 211-12.

37. Ibid., 214.

38. Ibid., 103-05.

39. Ibid., 220-22.

40. AFN website: <www.afn.ca/Fact%20Sheets/national_association_of_indigeno.htm>.

41. Special Senate Committee on Post-Secondary Education, *A Senate Report on Post-Secondary Education in Canada* (Ottawa: The Author, December 1997), 35-36.

42. Ibid., 34-35.

43. First Nations Adult and Higher Education Consortium website: <www.fnahec.org>.

44. "Indian Control of Indian Education Remains the Focus," *Windspeaker* (June 2000).

45. Vision Statement and other information available on website <www.afn.ca/Fact%20Sheets/national_association_of_indigeno.htm>.

46. *First Nations Messenger,* vol. 2, no. 5, Assembly of First Nations, Ottawa, Sept. 2000.

47. Assembly of First Nations, *Tradition and Education,* 50.

48. Del Anaquod, *Post-Secondary Education Study,* Touchwood/File Hills/Qu'Appelle Tribal Council, Fort Qu'Appelle, February 1990, 5.

49. Ibid., 84-94.

50. Indian And Northern Affairs Canada, *Post-Secondary Education Programs: A Cost/Benefit Assessment of Saskatchewan Indian Student Participation* (Regina: The Author, 1990), 3.

51. Federation of Saskatchewan Indian Nations, *Saskatchewan and Aboriginal Peoples in the 21st Century* (Regina: PrintWest, 1997), 32.

52. D. Ross, and P. Usher, *Education as an Investment for Treaty Indians in Saskatchewan: The Economic Costs and Benefits* (Saskatoon: Office of the Treaty Commissioner, 1992), 1-6.

53. Ibid., 6-8.

54. Ibid., 6-7.

55. Ibid., 20-22.

56. Ibid., 9-13.

57. Ibid., 10.

58. Indian and Northern Affairs Canada, *Post-Secondary Education for Status Indians and Inuit,* Ottawa, Nov. 1997, 1.

59. Indian Chiefs of Alberta, *Citizens Plus* (Edmonton: The Author, 1970), 34.

60. Assembly of First Nations, *Background Research for a Legal Opinion on Post-Secondary Education,* Ottawa, November 1991, 2.

61. Canadian Native Law Bulletin (CNLB), [1978] no. 4, 47–49, *Greyeyes v. The Queen,* Reported (1978) 84 DLR (3d) 196.

62. Assembly of First Nations, *Background Research,* 5-9.

63. Ibid., 1.

64. According to the legal opinion, those taking the position that post-secondary education is not a treaty right would have to prove that it was not intended to be part of a broadly interpreted treaty agreement, or that the government has intentionally abrogated that right. Federal funding of post-secondary education would suggest that the federal government has come to accept the principle of an Indian right to higher education.

65. Royal Commission on Aboriginal Peoples, *Public Policy and Aboriginal Peoples, 1965-1992* (Ottawa: Canada Communications Group, 1996), chapter 7.

66. Assembly of First Nations, *Tradition and Education,* vol. 2, 70.

67. Ibid., 149.

CHAPTER SIX

1. Dennis McPherson, and Douglas Rabb, "Restoring the Interpretive Circle: Community-Based Research and Education, *International Journal of Canadian Studies* 28 (Fall 2003): 157-58.

2. Ibid., 159.

3. Howard Adams, *Tortured People: The Politics of Colonization* (Penticton: Theytus Books, 1999), 54, cited in Dennis McPherson and Douglas Rabb, "Indigeneity in Canada: Spirituality, the Sacred and Survival," *International Journal of Canadian Studies* 23 (Spring 2001): 75.

4. McPherson and Rabb, "Indigeneity in Canada," 75.

5. Marie Battiste, and James Henderson, *Protecting Indigenous Knowledge and Heritage: A Global Challenge* (Saskatoon: Purich Publishing, 2000), 88-89.

6. Ibid., 520-21.

7.   RCAP, *Report,* vol. 3, 514-16.

8.   R.A. Malatest and Associates, "Best Practices in Increasing Aboriginal Post-secondary Enrolment Rates" (Ottawa: Canadian Council of Ministers of Education, 2002).

9.   Ibid., 45.

10. Ibid., 46.

11. Peter Nunoda, Access Coordinator, University of Manitoba, personal communication, 25 Apr. 2006.

12. *2003 Annual Education Report* at <www.manitobachiefs.com/education>.

13. The new name of the Saskatchewan Indian Federated College, First Nations University of Canada, was announced on 21 June 2003.

14. *Responsibilities and Education Jurisdiction,* at <www.cepn-fnec.com/juridic/resp>.

15. "Education Self-Government Agreement-in-Principle Reached with First Nations within the Anishinabek Nation", at <www.kahtou.com/images/selfeducation> (*Kahtou News* , 2000).

16. "Education Agreement in Principle", at <www.anishinabek.ca/ROJ/edu/gov-AIP.asp>.

17. Indian Governments of Saskatchewan, *An Act Respecting the Saskatchewan Indian Federated College,* 26 May 1994, 3.

18. Consortium website: <www.fnahec.org>.

19. *Aboriginal Post-Secondary Education and Training Policy Framework,* at <www.aved.gov.bc.ca/Aboriginal/framework>.

20. HRDC Canada at: <http://www11.hrsdc.gc.ca/en/cs/sp/hrsdc/edd/brief/1998-000593/feiig.shtml> (July 2006).

21. Assembly of First Nations, *National Review of First Nations Post-secondary Education Review* (Ottawa: The Author, 2000), 40.

22. Ibid., 42.

23. Hanson/Macleod Institute, 89, and Indian and Northern Affairs Canada, "Basic Departmental Data 2001," Ottawa, 2001.

24. Indian and Northern Affairs Canada at: <www.ainc-inac.gc.ca/nr/nwltr/sts/1996fs-9_e.html> (10 Sept. 2004).

25. DIAND Facts from stats, Issue m 17 Dec. 2000. Based on a population of 658,000 in 1998 and a 1.9% population growth rate.

26. Statistics Canada, at <www.statcan.ca/english/edu/clock/population.htm> (10 Sept. 2004). Based upon a 1 July 2004 population estimate of 31,900,034 and an annual growth rate of 0.855%.

27. Association of Universities and Colleges of Canada, *Quick Facts,* at <www.aucc.ca/publications/research/_quick_facts_e.html>. Of the students, 748,000 attend full-time and 280,000 part-time.

28. Association of Canadian Community Colleges, "Serving Communities", at <www.accc.ca/english/colleges/serving_communities.cfm>. Of these students, 900,000 are described as full-time and 1,500,000 as part-time learners.

29. National Chief Phil Fontaine's response to the Auditor General's recommendations on First Nations education, Assembly of First Nations website, at <www.afn.ca> (23 Nov. 2004).

30. *Government to Tax Aboriginal Post-Secondary Grants,* at <www.meadowlakeprogress.com/story.php?id=111107> (13 Sept. 2004).

31. Statistics Canada, *Universities and Colleges Revenue and Expenditure, Provinces and Territories,* at <www.statcan.ca/english/Pgdb/govt41a.htm> (13 Sept. 2002).

32. Statistics have been gleaned from university annual reports and from the Association of Universities and Colleges of Canada website <www.aucc.ca>. The enrolment of the First Nations University of Canada is an estimated full-time equivalent that includes class enrolments by University of Regina students. Total revenues include funds from all sources including tuitions, government transfers, capital, and restricted research funding. University enrolments may vary by year slightly, but the statistics are intended to portray a general analysis of funding per student.

33. According to Census Canada 2001 statistics, there were 976,305 Aboriginal people in Canada out of a total population of 29,639,035.

34. When community college post-secondary education is included, the amount of funding resources to which Aboriginal peoples should be entitled would more than double.

35. Assembly of First Nations, "Background Paper on Lifelong Learning," Ottawa, 20 Oct. 2004, 16.

36. Assembly of First Nations, *National Report of First Nations Post-secondary Education Review* (Ottawa: The Author, 2000), 12.

37. Assembly of First Nations/Indian and Northern Affairs Canada, *Draft Discussion Paper on Post-Secondary Education* (Ottawa: The Author, November 2001).

38. Chief Perry Bellegarde, "AFN Education Portfolio, to All First Nations Peoples," covering letter to the *National Report of First Nations Post-Secondary Review,* 25 Aug. 2000.

39. Liberal Party of Canada, *Creating Opportunity: The Liberal Plan for Canada* (Ottawa: The Author, 1993), 101; and covering letter to *National Report of First Nations Post-Secondary Education Review.*

40. AFN, "Background Paper on Lifelong Learning," October 2004, 16.

41. Council of Ministers of Higher Education, "Best Practices in Increasing Aboriginal Post-Secondary Enrolment Rates," May 2002, 25.

42. "Tribal Colleges Spread, Marking Slow Progress", at <www.newsday.com> (10 November. 2003).

43. Council of Ministers of Higher Education, "Best Practices," 29.

44. Institute for Higher Education Policy, "Tribal College Contributions to Local Economic Development," Washington, DC, 2000, 5–18.

45. Janet Holdsworth and Jenifer Dahlquist, "Tribal Community Colleges and On-Line Distance Education," paper presented at the 46th Conference for the Study of Community Colleges, April 2004.

46. Paul Boyer, "Native American Colleges: Progress and Prospects," Carnegie Foundation, 1997.

47. Marjane Ambler "Tribal Colleges Redefining Success," *Tribal College Journal* 16, 3 (Spring 2005).

48. *LeaderPost at* <www.canada.com/reginaleaderpost>, "Review Needed: Board Chair" (15 April 2005).

49. Pete Shauneen, Briefing Document to the Board of Governors, First Nations University of Canada, 8 May 2006.

50. *Leader-Post* at <www.canada.com/reginaleaderpost>, "University Given until Mid-June to Clean Up its Act" (15 Apr. 2006).

Bibliography

PRIMARY SOURCES

ARCHIVAL DOCUMENTS

Barber Papers, University of Regina Archives, Regina

Blakeney Papers, Saskatchewan Archives, Regina:

    GR238, file R565.

    R565, vii-110(f,), vii-110(h)

    R800, xliii, 64a(1)

Canada, *Sessional Papers* (on Microfiche at First Nations University of Canada Library)

Annual Report of Indian Affairs, 1886.

Annual Report of Indian Affairs, 1926.

Annual Report of Indian Affairs, 1927.

Annual Report of Indian Affairs, 1928.

Annual Report of Indian Affairs, 1958.

Annual Report of Indian Affairs, 1961.

Annual Report of Indian Affairs, 1964.

National Archives of Canada (NAC) Ottawa, Record Group 10:

    Volume 3122, File 330, 203.

    Volume 3159, File 359.

    Volume 3710, File 19, 550-3.

    Volume 3932, File 117,504-1

National Archives of Canada, Sir John A. Macdonald Papers, Vol. 107.

National Archives of Canada, Manuscript Group 26, Dewdney Papers.

Treaties and Historical Centre, Indian and Northern Affairs, Gatineau, Quebec:

    File 1/25-22-30, Volume 30

    File 1/25-22-30, Volume 31

    File A119725

    File A126715

    File A147452

    File A153805

File A175137

File E-4727-1

File K217163

File NARC 5-119

File N145123

GOVERNMENT PUBLICATIONS AND POLICY PAPERS

Auditor General of Canada. *Report of the Auditor General for the period ending March 31*, 1986. Ottawa.

____. *Report of the Auditor General for the period ending March 31, 1988.* Ottawa.

Canada. *British North America Act* (1867).

____. *Constitution Act* (1982).

____. Federal Policy Guide: Aboriginal Self-Goverment. Ottawa: Indian Affairs and Northern Development (1995).

____. Joint Committee of the Senate and House of Commons on Indian Affairs. *Final Report* to Parliament, 1961.

____. Privy Council Office. *Consensus Report on the Constitution.* 28 August 1992.

____. *Statement of the Government of Canada on Indian Policy.* Ottawa, 1969.

Government of British Columbia. "Aboriginal Post-Secondary Education and Training Policy Framework." Ministry of Advanced Education, 1995.

Hanson/Macleod Institute. *Post-Secondary Evaluation: Draft Consolidated Report.* Ottawa : Indian and Northern Affairs Canada, 2003.

House of Commons. *Debates,* 46 Vict. (1883). *Debates* (1974).

____. Standing Committee on Indian Affairs and Northern Development. *Minutes of Proceedings and Evidence.* 24 May 1973.

____. *Report of the Standing Committee on Aboriginal Affairs and Northern Development, Sub-Committee on Aboriginal Education.* Ottawa, 1996.

____. Standing Committee on Aboriginal Affairs. *A Review of the Post-Secondary Student Assistance Program of the Department of Indian Affairs and Northern Development.* Ottawa, 1989.

____. Standing Committee on Indian Affairs. *Basic Departmental Data.* Indian and Northern Affairs Canada, 1989.

Hull, Jeremy. Aboriginal Post-Secondary Education and Labour Market Outcomes, 1996. Gatineau: Indian and Northern Affairs Canada, 2000.

____. An Overview of the Educational Characteristics of Registered Indians in Canada. Ottawa: Indian Affairs and Northern Development, 1987.

Indian Act. Revised Statutes of Canada, 1970.

Indian Affairs. Annual Reports, 1958–63. Ottawa: Queen's Printer.

Indian Affairs. Working Committee on Manitou College. Minutes. 18–19 February 1975.

Indian and Northern Affairs Canada. *The Indian and Inuit Graduate Register.* Ottawa: Indian and Eskimo Program, 1976.

____. *Evaluation of the Post-Secondary Education Assistance Program.* Ottawa: Evaluation Directorate, 1989.

____. *Post-Secondary Education Assistance Evaluation Study.* Ottawa: Evaluation Branch, 1985.

____. *Post-Secondary Education for Status Indians and Inuit.* Hull: Indian and Northern Affairs, 1997.

____. *Post-Secondary Education Programs: A Cost-Benefit Assessment of Saskatchewan Indian Participation.* Regina, 1990.

____. *Post-Secondary Student Support Program Terms of Reference.* Gatineau: Audit and Evaluation Branch, 2002.

____. *University Education and Economic Well-Being: Indian Achievement and Prospects.* Ottawa: Quantitative Analysis and Socio-Demographic Research, 1990.

Jenness, Diamond. *Plan for Liquidating Canada's Indian Problem within 25 Years.* Minutes of Proceedings and Evidence, Special Joint Committee of the Senate and House of Commons on the Indian Act, 25 March 1947.

R.A. Malatest and Associates. "Best Practices in Increasing Aboriginal Post-Secondary Enrolment Rates." Canadian Council of Ministers of Education, 2002.

____. "Aboriginal Peoples and Post-secondary Education: What Educators Have Learned." Canadian Millenium Scholarship Foundation, 2004.

Saskatchewan Education. *A Five Year Action Plan for Native Curriculum Development.* Regina: Government of Saskatchewan, 1984.

____. *Reaching Out: The Report of the Indian and Metis Consultations.* Regina: Government of Saskatchewan, 1985.

Saskatchewan Human Rights Commission. *Education Equity: A Report on Indian/ Native Education in Saskatchewan.* Regina: Human Rights Commission, 1985.

Special Senate Committee on Post-Secondary Education. *A Senate Report on Post-Secondary Education in Canada.* Ottawa: Senate of Canada, 1997.

FIRST NATIONS DOCUMENTS

Aboriginal Institute of Canada. "Flim Flam or Now You See It Now You Don't: The 42 Million Dollar Cultural Education Program." Ottawa, 1976.

Aboriginal Institutes Consortium, Ontario, *Annual Report*, 2001–2002.

Ambler, Marjane, "Tribal Colleges Redefining Success." *The Tribal College Journal* 16, 3 (Spring 2005).

Anaquod, Del. *Post-Secondary Education Study.* Fort Qu'Appelle: Touchwood/ File Hills/Qu'Appelle Tribal Council, 1990.

____. and Donna Pinay. "An Historical Overview of the Saskatchewan Indian Federated College 1976–1998." Unpublished document. Regina, 1998.

Assembly of First Nations. "Background Research for a Legal Opinion on Post-Secondary Education." Unpublished document. Ottawa: Education Secretariat, 1991.

____. "Background Paper on Lifelong Learning." Ottawa. 20 October 2004.

____. *Breaking the Silence.* Ottawa: First Nations Health Commission, 1994.

____. "National Review of First Nations Post-secondary Education," Ottawa, 2000.

____. *Tradition and Education: Towards a Vision of Our Future.* Ottawa: Assembly of First Nations, 1988.

Federation of Saskatchewan Indian Nations. *Saskatchewan and Aboriginal Peoples in the 21st Century.* Regina: PrintWest, 1997.

Federation of Saskatchewan Indians. "Principles of Indian Government." Unpublished document. Regina, 1977.

____. *Annual Report.* Saskatoon: Federation of Saskatchewan Indians, 1997.

Holdsworth, Janet, and Jenifer Dahlquist. "Tribal Community Colleges and On-Line Distance Education." Paper presented at the 46th Conference for the Study of Community Colleges, April 2004.

Indian Association of Alberta. "Proposed Revisions to the Indian Act." Edmonton, 1974.

Indian Chiefs of Alberta. *Citizens Plus.* Edmonton: Indian Association of Alberta, 1970.

Institute for Higher Education Policy. "Tribal College Contributions to Local Economic Development." Washington, DC, 2000.

National Indian Brotherhood. *Indian Control of Indian Education.* Ottawa: The Author, 1972.

National Indian Education Forum and Alexander School Board. *Interim Recommended Changes to the Post-Secondary Student Assistance Program.* Morinville AB, 1989.

Native North American Studies Institute. Board of Governors Meeting, 9 November 1973.

Saskatchewan Indian Federated College. Academic Calendar, 1998–2000.

____. "Briefing Notes for Meeting with the Cabinet." Government of Saskatchewan, 31 January 1997.

Saskatchewan Indian Cultural College. *Indian Education in Saskatchewan.* 3 vols. Saskatoon: Federation of Saskatchewan Indians, 1973.

Stonechild, Blair: Personal Collection.

____. Manitou Community College, *Academic Report,* 21 March 1975.

____. Manitou Community College, Calendar 1974–1975.

____. Manitou Community College, *Financial Report to the Indians of Quebec Association to August 23, 1974.*

____. Manitou Community College, *Status Report to Assistant Deputy Minister of Indian Affairs,* 14 December 1973.

____. Manitou Community College: *Progress Report,* November 1973–August 1974.

____. Manitou Community College: *Recruiting Report for Ontario,* 2-29 November 1974.

Swain, Marcel. "Background Research for a Legal Opinion on Post-Secondary Education." Assembly of First Nations, Ottawa, 1991.

NEWSPAPERS

First Nations Messenger
  September 2000
Globe and Mail
Leader-Post
Ottawa Citizen 1968
Saskatchewan Indian
  September 1987
  September 1988
  March 1989
  April 1989
  September 1989
Windspeaker
  June 2000

INTERVIEWS AND COMMUNICATIONS

Sheppard, Bruce. Past Director, Diefenbaker Centre, Saskatoon, 22 October 2003.

Starblanket, Noel. Former President, National Indian Brotherhood, Fort Qu'Appelle, 16 April 2003.

Star-Spaeth, Danette. Director of Higher Education, Federation of Saskatchewan Indian Nations, Regina, 7 October 2002.

Valaskakis, Gail. Research Director, Aboriginal Healing Foundation, Ottawa, 18 April 2002.

SECONDARY SOURCES

Association of Canadian Community Colleges. *Meeting the Needs of Aboriginal Learners.* Ottawa: Association of Canadian Community Colleges, 2005.

Barman, Jean, Yvonne Hebert, and Don McCaskill. *Indian Education in Canada: The Legacy.* Vancouver: University of British Columbia Press, 1986.

Barron, Laurie. *Walking in Indian Moccasins: The Native Policies of Tommy Douglas and the CCF.* Vancouver: University of British Columbia Press, 1977.

Battiste, Marie, and Jean Barman. *First Nations Education in Canada: The Circle Unfolds.* Vancouver: University of British Columbia Press, 1995.

Battiste, Marie, and James Henderson. *Protecting Indigenous Knowledge and Heritage: A Global Challenge.* Saskatoon: Purich Publishing, 2000.

Beal, Bob, and Rod Macleod. *Prairie Fire.* Edmonton: Hurtig Publishing, 1984.

Bercuson, David, Robert Bothwell, and Jack Granatstein. *Petrified Campus: The Crisis in Canada's Universities.* Toronto: Random House, 1997.

Boldt, Menno. *Surviving as Indians: The Challenge of Self-Government.* Toronto: University of Toronto, 1993.

Boulton, Marsha. *Just a Minute More.* Toronto: McArthur and Co, 1999.

Brooks, Stephen. *Public Policy in Canada: An Introduction.* Toronto: McClelland and Stewart, 1993.

Brooks, Stephen, and David Easton. *A Systems Analysis of Political Life.* New York: John Wiley and Sons, 1965.

Bryce, Peter. *The Story of a National Crime: An Appeal for Justice to the Indians of Canada.* Ottawa: James Hope and Sons, 1922.

Cairns, Alan. *Citizens Plus: Aboriginal Peoples and the Canadian State.* Vancouver: University of British Columbia Press, 2000.

Cardinal, Harold. *The Unjust Society.* Edmonton: Hurtig Publishing, 1969.

_____. *The Rebirth of Canada's Indians.* Edmonton: Hurtig Publishing, 1977.

Carter, Sarah. *Lost Harvests: Prairie Indian Reserve Farmers and Government Policy.* Montreal: McGill-Queen's University Press, 1990.

Castellano, Marlene, Lynn Davis, and Louise Lahache. *Aboriginal Education: Fulfilling the Promise.* Vancouver: University of British Columbia Press, 2000.

Cisneros, Wanda. "Native Education in Quebec: A Report to the Challenge for Change Division of the National Film Board." Unpublished document, n.d.

Clarkson, B. *Functional Health Plan for Indians in the North Battleford Area.* Ottawa: Medical Services Branch, 1977.

Creighton, Donald. *John A. Macdonald: The Old Chieftain.* Toronto: McMillan, 1965.

Cumming, Peter, and Neil Mickenberg, eds. *Native Rights in Canada.* Toronto: Indian-Eskimo Association of Canada, 1972.

Dempsey, Hugh. *Big Bear: The End of Freedom.* Vancouver: Douglas and McIntyre, 1984.

Dickason, Olive. *Canada's First Nations, A History of Founding People from Earliest Times.* Toronto: Oxford University Press, 1997.

Dyck, Rand. *Canadian Politics: Critical Approaches.* 2nd ed. Toronto: Nelson Canada (1996).

Easton, David. *A Systems Analysis of Political Life.* New York: John Wiley and Sons, 1965.

English, John. *The Worldly Years: The Life of Lester Pearson, 1949-1972.* Toronto: Vintage Books, 1993.

Evalucan Ltd. "Evaluation of the Cultural Education Centres Program." Calgary: Evalucan, 1978.

Flanagan, Tom. *First Nations, Second Thoughts.* Montreal: McGill-Queen's University Press, 2000.

Frideres, James. *Aboriginal Peoples in Canada: Contemporary Conflicts.* 5th ed. Scarborough: Prentice Hall Allyn, 1998.

Fumoleau, René. *As Long as This Land Shall Last.* Toronto: McClelland and Stewart, 1975.

Getty, Ian, and Antoine Lussier. *As Long as the Sun Shines and Waters Flow.* Vancouver: University of British Columbia Press, 1983.

Hawkes, M. *Social Darwinism in European and American Thought 1860-1945.* New York: Cambridge University Press, 1997.

Hawthorn, Harry B., et al. *A Survey of Contemporary Indians of Canada: Economic, Political, Educational Needs and Policies.* 2 vols. Ottawa: Queen's Printer, 1966.

Hayden, Michael. *The University of Saskatchewan 1907–1982.* Vancouver: University of British Columbia Press, 1983.

Hofdstader, Richard. *Social Darwinism in American Thought.* New York: George Braziller, 1959.

Hogg, Peter. *Constitutional Law of Canada.* Toronto: Carswell, 1998.

Holmes, David. *Redressing the Balance: Canadian University Programs in Support of Aboriginal Students.* Ottawa: Association of Universities and Colleges of Canada, 2006.

Horseman, Reginald. *Race and Manifest Destiny: The Origins of American Racial Anglo-Saxonism.* Cambridge: Harvard University Press, 1981.

Houston, Stuart. *R.G. Ferguson: Crusader Against Tuberculosis.* Toronto: Dundurn Press, 1991.

Hylton, John. *Aboriginal Self-Government in Canada.* Saskatoon: Purich Publishing, 1999.

Jenness, Diamond. *Plan for Liquidating Canada's Indian Problem within 25 Years.* Ottawa: Special Joint Committee of the House of Commons and Senate on Indian Affairs, 1947.

Jones, Glen A., ed. *Higher Education in Canada: Different Systems, Different Perspectives.* New York: Garland Publishing, 1997.

Katenies Research and Management Services. *Review of the Indian Studies Support Program Component of PSE.* Sackville: Chignecto Consulting Group, 2006.

Kelm, Mary-Ellen. *Colonizing Bodies: Aboriginal Health and Healing in British Columbia, 1900–50.* Vancouver: University of British Columbia Press, 1998.

Kulchyski, Peter. *Unjust Relations: Aboriginal Rights in Canadian Courts.* Toronto: Oxford University Press, 1994.

Laliberte, Ron, Priscilla Settee, et al., eds. *Expressions in Canadian Native Studies.* Saskatoon: University of Saskatchewan, 2000.

Little Bear, Leroy, Menno Boldt, and Anthony Long. *Pathways to Self-Determination: Canadian Indians and the Canadian State.* Toronto: University of Toronto Press, 1984.

Long, Anthony, and Menno Boldt, eds. *Governments in Conflict: Provinces and Indian Nations in Canada.* Toronto: University of Toronto Press, 1988.

Manuel, George. *The Fourth World: An Indian Reality.* New York: Collier-Macmillan, 1974.

McCall, C., and S. Clarkson, *Trudeau and Our Times.* Vol. 2. Toronto: McClelland and Stewart, 1990.

McFarlane, Peter. *Brotherhood to Nationhood: George Manuel and the Making of the Modern Indian Movement.* Toronto: Between the Lines, 1993.

McKechnie, Robert. *Strong Medicine: History of Healing on the North-West Coast.* Vancouver: J.J. Douglas, 1972.

Mercredi, Ovide, and Mary Ellen Turpel. *In the Rapids: Navigating the Future of First Nations.* Toronto: Viking, 1993.

Mihesuah, Devon, ed. *Natives and Academics: Researching and Writing about American Indians.* Lincoln: University of Nebraska Press, 1998.

Miller, J.R. *Skyscrapers Hide the Heavens.* Toronto: University of Toronto Press, 1989.

_____. *Shingwauk's Vision: A History of Native Residential Schools.* Toronto: University of Toronto Press, 1996.

Milloy, John. *A National Crime: The Canadian Government and the Residential School System.* Winnipeg: University of Manitoba Press, 1999.

Morris, Alexander. *The Treaties of Canada with the Indians of Manitoba and the North-West Territories.* Toronto: Coles, 1979. Reprint.

Morton, Arthur. *Saskatchewan: Making of a University.* Toronto: University of Toronto Press, 1959.

Native North American Studies Institute. *First Peoples in Quebec.* 3 vols. LaMacaza: Thunderbird Press, 1973.

Obomsawin, R. *Traditional Indian Health and Nutrition.* Ottawa: National Indian Brotherhood, 1979.

Office of the Treaty Commissioner. *Education as an Investment for Treaty Indians in Saskatchewan: The Economic Costs and Benefits.* Saskatoon: The Author, 1992.

Opikokew, Delia. *The First Nations: Indian Government and the Canadian Confederation.* Saskatoon: Federation of Saskatchewan Indians, 1980.

Patterson, Palmer. *The Canadian Indian: A History since 1500.* Don Mills: Collier-Macmillan, 1972.

Pettipas, Katherine. *Severing the Ties that Bind: Government Repression of Indigenous Religious Ceremonies on the Prairies.* Winnipeg: University of Manitoba Press, 1994.

Pitsula, James. *An Act of Faith: The Early Years of Regina College.* Regina: Canadian Plains Research Centre, 1988.

Ponting, Rick, and Roger Gibbins. *Out of Irrelevance.* Scarborough: Butterworth, 1980.

Pross, Paul A. *Group Politics and Public Policy.* 2nd ed. Toronto: Oxford University Press, 1992.

Purich, Don. *Our Land, Native Rights in Canada.* Toronto: Lorimer, 1986.

Ray, Arthur, Jim Miller, and Frank Tough. *Bounty and Benevolence: A History of Saskatchewan Treaties.* Montreal: McGill-Queen's University Press, 2000.

Riddell, William A. *The First Decade: A History of the University of Regina, Saskatchewan Campus 1960–1970.* Regina: University of Regina Press, 1974.

Riel, Louis. *The Complete Writings of Louis Riel.* Edmonton: University of Alberta Press, 1985.

Royal Commission on Aboriginal Peoples. *Path to Healing: Report of the National Round Table on Aboriginal Health and Social Issues.* Ottawa: Canada Communications Group, 1993.

_____. *Report.* 5 vols. Ottawa: Canada Communications Group, 1995.

Schwartz, Bryan. *First Principles, Second Thoughts: Aboriginal Peoples, Constitutional Reform and Canadian Statecraft.* Montreal: Institute for Research on Public Policy, 1986.

Sluman, Norma, and Jean Goodwill. *John Tootoosis—A Biography.* Ottawa: Golden Dog Press, 1982.

Smith, Stuart. *Report of the Commission of Inquiry on Canadian University Education.* Ottawa: Association of Universities and Colleges of Canada, 1991.

Smith, Denis. *Rogue Tory: The Life and Legend of John G. Diefenbaker.* Toronto: MacFarlane, Walter and Ross, 1995.

Smith, Linda Tuhiwai. *Decolonizing Methodologies: Research and Indigenous Peoples.* New York: Zed Books, 1999.

Stevenson, P., S. Elliot, L. Foster, and J. Harris, eds. *A Persistent Spirit: Towards Understanding Aboriginal Health in British Columbia.* Victoria: University of Victoria Press, 1995.

Stonechild, Blair, and Bill Waiser. *Loyal Till Death, Indians and the North-West Rebellion.* Calgary: Fifth House, 1997.

Thornton, Russell. *American Indian Holocaust and Survival.* Norman: University of Oklahoma Press, 1987.

Titley, Brian. *A Narrow Vision: Duncan Campbell Scott and the Administration of Indian Affairs in Canada.* Vancouver: University of British Columbia Press, 1986.

Thompson, W.P. *The University of Saskatchewan: A Personal History.* Toronto: University of Toronto Press, 1970.

Venne, Sharon. *Indian Acts and Amendments 1868-1975.* Saskatoon: Native Law Centre, 1981.

Waldram, James, Ann Herring, and Kue Young. *Aboriginal Health in Canada: Historical, Cultural and Epidemiological Perspectives.* Toronto: University of Toronto Press, 1985.

Waubageshig. *The Only Good Indian.* Toronto: New Press, 1970.

Weaver, Sally. *Making Canadian Indian Policy: The Hidden Agenda, 1968-70.* Toronto: University of Toronto Press, 1981.

Wherrett, George. *The Miracle of Empty Beds: A History of Tuberculosis in Canada.* Toronto: University of Toronto Press, 1977.

Wotherspoon, Terry. *Hitting the Books: The Politics of Educational Retrenchment.* Toronto: Garamond Press, 1991.

Wuttunee, William. *Ruffled Feathers: Indians in Canadian Society.* Calgary: Bell Publishing, 1971.

Young, D., G. Ingram, and L. Schwarz, L. *Cry of the Eagle: Encounters with a Cree Healer.* Toronto: University of Toronto Press, 1977.

Young, T. Kue. *The Health of the Native Americans: Toward a Biocultural Epidemiology.* New York: Oxford University Press, 1994.

ARTICLES

Anaquod, Del, and Donna Pinay. "An Historical Overview of the Saskatchewan Indian Federated College." Unpublished document. November 1998.

Alaska Native Knowledge Network. "Who is this Child named WIPCE [World Indigenous Peoples Conference on Education]." *Sharing Our Pathways* 7,4 (2002).

Atkinson, Michael, and William Coleman. "Policy Networks, Policy Communities and the Problem of Governance." In *Policy Studies in Canada,* ed. L. Dobuzinsky, M. Howlett, and D. Laycock. Toronto: University of Toronto Press, 1996.

Barkwell, P.A. "The Medicine Chest Clause in Treaty Number Six." *Canadian Native Law Reporter* (1981).

Barnhardt, Ray. "Higher Education in the Fourth World: Indigenous People Take Control." *Canadian Journal of Native Education* 18, 2 (1991).

Basran, G.S. "History and Rationale of the Affirmative Action Program, College of Arts and Science, University of Saskatchewan." *Canadian Journal of Native Studies* X, 2 (1990)

Boyer, Paul. "Native American Colleges: Progress and Prospects." Carnegie Foundation, 1997.

Couture, Joe. "Native Studies and the Academy." In Sefa Dei, G., B. Hall, and D. Rosenberg D., *Indigenous Knowledges in Global Contexts.* Toronto: University of Toronto Press, 2000.

de Valk, A. "Independent University of Federated College?" *Saskatchewan History* xxx (1977)

Green, Joyce. "Self-Determination, Citizenship and Federalism: Indigenous and Canadian Palimpsest." Saskatchewan Institute of Public Policy, Regina. 2003.

Hampton, Eber. "First Nations-Controlled University Education in Canada." In M. Castellano, L. Davis, and L. Lahache, *Aboriginal Education: Fulfilling the Promise.* Vancouver: University of British Columbia Press, 2000.

Hampton, Eber, and Steve Wolfson. "Education for Self-Determination." In Hylton, John, *Aboriginal Self-Government in Canada.* Saskatoon: Purich Publishing, 1999.

Howlett, Michael. "Policy Paradigms and Policy Change: Lessons from the Old and New Canadian Policies Towards Aboriginal Peoples." *Policy Studies Journal* 22, 4 (1994).

"Implications for Post-Secondary Education: The Saskatchewan Indian Federated College Response to the New Post-secondary Student Assistance Program." *Saskatchewan Indian Federated College Journal* 4, 2 (1988).

Indian Claims Commission. "An Essay, Research Resource Centre." Ottawa: The Author, 1975.

_____. "Rouseau River Anishinabe First Nation Inquiry." 14 ICCP (2001), Ottawa.

Lanceley, Darlene. "The Post-Secondary Assistance Program for Indian Education: The Vehicle for Change and the Voice of Opposition." In Wotherspoon, Terry, *Hitting the Books.* Toronto: Garamound Press, 1991.

Kirkness, Verna. "Native Teachers, A Key to Progress." *Canadian Journal of Native Education (1986).*

Leighton, Douglas. "A Victorian Civil Servant at Work: Lawrence Vankoughnet and the Canadian Indian Department 1874-1893." In Getty, A. and A. Lussier, *As Long as the Sun Shines and Waters Flow.* Vancouver: University of British Columbia Press, 1983.

McCaskill, Don, and Blair Stonechild. "The Development of Native Studies in Canada." In *Education, Research and Information Systems and the North,* ed. P. Adams. Ottawa: Association of Universities for Northern Development, 1978.

McLeod, Neal. "Indigenous Studies: Negotiating the Space Between Tribal Communities and Academia." In Laliberte, Ron, Priscilla Settee et al., *Expressions in Canadian Native Studies*. Saskatoon: University of Saskatchewan Press, 2000.

McPherson, Dennis and Douglas Rabb. "Indigeneity in Canada: Spirituality, the Sacred and Survival." *International Journal of Canadian Studies* 23 (Spring 2001).

____. "Restoring the Interpretive Circle: Community-Based Research and Education." *International Journal of Canadian Studies* 28 (Fall 2003).

Pitsula, James. "The Saskatchewan CCF Government and Treaty Indians." *Canadian Historical Review* LXXV, 1 (1994).

____. "The Saskatchewan Government and Treaty Indians, 1944-64." *Canadian Historical Review* LXXV, 1 (1994).

____. "The Thatcher Government in Saskatchewan and Treaty Indians, 1964-1971." *Saskatchewan History* (Spring 1996).

Saskatchewan Indian Cultural Centre. "A Commentary on the History of Cultural-Educational Centres Funding." Saskatoon, nd.

Spencer, Herbert. "Progress: Its Law and Causes." *Westminster Review* 67 (April 1857).

Stevenson, Winona. "Prairie Indians and Higher Education: An Historical Overview 1876-1977." In Wothersoon, Terry, *Hitting the Books*. Toronto: Garamond Press, 1991.

Taylor, Donald, Martha Crago, and Lynne Alpine. "Education in Aboriginal Communities: Dilemmas around Empowerment." *Canadian Journal of Native Education (1993).*

Titley, Brian. "The League of Indians of Canada: An Early Attempt to Create a National Native Organization." *Saskatchewan Indian Federated College Journal* 1, 1 (1984).

Tobias, John. "Protection, Civilization, Assimilation: An Outline History of Canada's Indian Policy." *Western Canadian Journal of Anthropology* 6, 2 (1976).

University of Saskatchewan. "Indians and the University." *The Green and White: The University of Saskatchewan Alumni Association Magazine* (Winter 1973).

Weaver, Sally. "Indian Policy in the New Conservative Government, Part 1: The Nielsen Task Force of 1985." *Native Studies Review* 2, 1 (1986).

____. "The Joint Cabinet/National Indian Brotherhood Committee: A Unique Experiment in Pressure Group Relations." *Canadian Public Administration* 25 (Summer 1982).

Websters's University Dictionary. Boston: Houghton-Mifflin (1988).

THESES

Craig, Barbara. "Jurisdiction in Aboriginal Health in Canada. LLM Thesis, University of Ottawa, 1997.

Leslie, John. "Assimilation, Integration or Termination? The Development of Canadian Indian Policy, 1943-1963." PhD Thesis, Carleton University, 1999.

Stonechild, Blair. "Pursuing the New Buffalo: First Nations Post-Secondary Policy in Canada." PhD Thesis, University of Regina, 2004.

Taylor, John Leonard. "The Development of an Indian Policy for the Canadian North-West, 1869–79." PhD Thesis, Queen's University, 1975.

Thaner, Shona. "The Development of Native Studies at Canadian Universities: Four Programs, Four Provinces, Four Decades." MA Thesis, Carleton University, 1997.

Ward, Margaret S. "Indian Education in Canada: Implementation of Indian Policy, 1973–1978." MEd Thesis, University of Saskatchewan, 1988.

INTERNET SOURCES

Assembly of First Nations. <www.afn.ca>

Assembly of Manitoba Chiefs. <www.manitobachiefs.com>

Association of Canadian Community Colleges. <www.accc.ca>

Association of Universities and Colleges of Canada. <www.aucc.ca>

First Nations Adult and Higher Education Consortium. <www.fnahec.org>

First Nations Educational Council. <www.cepn-fnec.com>

First Nations University of Canada. <www.firstnationsuniversity.ca>

Human Resources and Social Development Canada. <www.hrdc-drhc.gc.ca>

Indian and Northern Affairs Canada. <www.ainc-inac.gc.ca>

Kahtou News. <www.kahtou.com>

Meadow Lake Progress. <www.meadowlakeprogress.com>

Newsday.com. <www.newsday.com>

Province of British Columbia. <www./aved.gov.bc.ca>

Regina Leader-Post. <www.canada.com>

Statistics Canada. <www.statscan.ca>

University of Saskatchewan. <www.usask.ca>

Index